EVERYONE IS
REDEEMABLE

DAILY DEVOTIONAL

Downtown Women's Center

SERVING THE HOMELESS SINCE 1989

DOWNTOWN WOMEN'S CENTER

WESTBOW
PRESS®
A DIVISION OF THOMAS NELSON
& ZONDERVAN

WestBow Press books may be ordered through booksellers or by contacting:

WestBow Press
A Division of Thomas Nelson & Zondervan
1663 Liberty Drive
Bloomington, IN 47403
www.westbowpress.com
844-714-3454

ISBN: 979-8-3850-1285-5 (sc)
ISBN: 979-8-3850-1286-2 (hc)
ISBN: 979-8-3850-1284-8 (e)

Library of Congress Control Number: 2023922252

Print information available on the last page.

WestBow Press rev. date: 11/22/2023

TO SISTER MARY VIRGINIA CLARK, DC

Affectionately known throughout her lifetime as "Ginny Girl" by her many siblings, Sister Mary Virginia (baptized Virginia Dolores) was born on April 3, 1926, in Webster Groves, Missouri (a suburb of St. Louis). Her parents were Harry Freeman and Ellen Catherine (Hurley) Clark.

"Ginny Girl" was a playful, mischievous, and energetic girl and remained so as a Daughter of Charity. Many stories recount her playful nature, energy, and vision, which is evident in the establishment of the Downtown Women's Center. She was touched dramatically by God's beauty in her family life and strived to offer beauty in music and art to the struggling women she served. Ginny Girl's musician mother nurtured all of her children with visual art and music, despite their family's financial struggles.

Sister Mary Virginia graduated from Visitation Academy in St. Louis in 1943. She entered the Daughters of Charity from Holy Redeemer Catholic Church in Webster Groves in September 1947. She earned her bachelor of arts in education from Fontbonne College (now University) in St. Louis (1955). Sister continued her studies while teaching; she earned her master of education degree in administration and supervision from Loyola University in New Orleans (1964) and her master of arts degree in theology and counseling from Manhattanville College in Purchase, New York (1968).

Sister Mary Virginia Clark led a humble life, serving the poor and marginalized. She had the vision to provide shelter and spiritual guidance to homeless women and children. In 1989, that dream was realized with the purchase of two old houses and the founding of the Downtown Women's Center (DWC) in Amarillo, Texas. Her legacy runs deep throughout the DWC. She is remembered and honored by the traditions she began. A favorite tradition is the Nativity scene. Sister didn't want baby Jesus to be placed in his crib until Christmas Day. Each year, a special person is assigned to deliver Jesus to the manger early on Christmas morning.

1989

2022

The Daughters of Charity wore simple light-blue skirts and jackets, but Sister Mary Virginia loved color. She enjoyed beautiful flowers, and the food she prepared was both delicious and colorful. Sister wanted every woman and child to experience life's colors through cultural activities. She believed, "The poor deserve beauty too." DWC adheres to that sentiment by providing cultural activities as part of the recovery program—activities that the women and their children may never have experienced. She believed that they should know that *life can be very beautiful.*

Sister's joy for life was the fruit of her love for God and all people, especially for the homeless women and children that DWC is called and blessed to serve. She lived her life believing, "Kindness shown to the poor is an act of worship" (Proverbs 14:31 GNT).

Sister Mary Virginia died March 27, 2020, at Seton Residence, Evansville, Indiana. She was ninety-three years of age and had spent seventy-two years as a Daughter of Charity of St. Vincent de Paul. On March 30, 2020, she was laid to rest, as she lived her life, humbly and in the presence of God. No one was in attendance due to COVID-19 restrictions.

Sister Mary Virginia, your legacy lives on. You are loved.

MONSIGNOR HAROLD WALDOW

Thank you, Monsignor Waldow, for your countless hours of prayer and dedication to the mission and vision of the Downtown Women's Center. Thank you for seeing us through the bad times and the good times, always having faith that God would provide. Thank you for your selfless acts of generosity, both physically and spiritually, to the women and children of DWC. Thank you for knowing that the power of God is greater than any power of addiction. Thank you for loving and blessing the Downtown Women's Center since we began. Thank you for being "just one of the girls."

Your spirit will forever be with the Downtown Women's Center.

FOREWORD

Three thousand eighty-four days ago, Cassandra lost her sister, and we lost our daughter. But who's counting? Three thousand two days ago, we noticed a stark difference in Cassandra's behavior. Who was she becoming? Two thousand five hundred eighty-six days ago, my young son brought us a cup with a syringe in it that he found in his bedroom. At that point, we knew Cassandra could no longer live in our home; that is when the chaos began. But who's counting? One thousand two hundred sixty-one days ago, Cassandra called and told us a drug dealer had just beaten her up; she was dragged behind his car and was afraid to call the police or the ambulance because she had issues. My wife and I had to dress her wounds, and this was just part of our lives at this point. But again, who's counting? Nine hundred thirty-two days ago, Cassandra was sleeping on the streets. She was using a curb as a pillow, and she called me and said, "Daddy, please take me to Lubbock. I want to go into the rehab facility there." But who's counting? Nine hundred fourteen days ago, she was dismissed from that rehab facility. Eight hundred forty-two days ago, she was admitted into an intermediate sanction facility for six months. But again, who's counting? Seven hundred seventeen days ago, she was released from that facility. But again, who's counting? Seven hundred four days ago, Cassandra started using again. But again, who's counting?

Our daughter started her journey back home 592 days ago by entering the Downtown Women's Center. We have our daughter back! That is when we started counting. Not only counting the days of her sobriety, but we started counting on Cassandra being who she is. We started counting on Haven House. We started counting on her counselors, and we started counting on Cassandra being the human being that she is today. We are so incredibly grateful for the Downtown Women's Center. God bless Haven House. God bless ARAD. God bless drug court. God bless Gratitude House. And God bless Downtown Women's Center.

This book shows the strength of addiction, the darkness, the hopelessness, and how it can destroy not only the life of the one who is addicted but how it affects their whole family. This book also shows the strength of God, the power of hope, and the power of love. We can all find a piece of ourselves or our family in these stories. Let us draw inspiration from the women who have passed through the Downtown Women's Center and remember that everything is possible through God. Through God, everyone is redeemable.

—Tom, Cassandra's dad

PREFACE

The Downtown Women's Center's daily devotional was written and edited during the COVID-19 pandemic. It takes great courage for our ladies to tell their stories, especially when the story is of addiction, hopelessness, bad choices, and finally being redeemed, by the grace of God, through recovery. This book is written in memory of our founder and director for eleven years, Sister Mary Virginia Clark. Women and men will enjoy this daily devotional of encouragement and redemption.

ACKNOWLEDGMENTS

We celebrate all the women, men, and children who have passed through our doors. Their triumphs over addiction and homelessness inspire the community to reach out to help DWC and those we serve. Because of their willingness to share their stories, this book will help touch and redeem countless more lives.

INTRODUCTION

Substance use disorders often stem from childhood and adult physical and sexual abuse. Behavioral health disorders may also lead individuals to self-medicate with intoxicants. In either case, the individual seeks an escape from intolerable conditions through substance use. Instead of escape, however, the drugs just entrap the individual in another, often-more-dreadful condition.

Addiction is so powerful. A mother of a precious child once told me she would take a bullet for her son, but she couldn't stop using drugs for him. How cunning, baffling, and powerful addiction truly is! Addiction is a life-threatening, crippling disorder that impacts the entire family. The family often suffers years of indescribable worry, heartache, and even anger. They may exhaust their financial resources. These families are in constant prayer for the loved one they don't really know anymore.

When a family realizes that they can't keep doing the same things and hoping for different results, tough love provides a difficult but compassionate approach. God gives us strength to do the next right thing—at the right time. For the person we love more than life itself, we learn to finally say no and to stop enabling bad choices and dangerous behaviors.

Individuals with addiction often blame everyone around them for their problems. They continue their risky lifestyles until something powerful—sometimes terrible—gets their attention. For some, incarceration is the wake-up call. For others, experiencing a near-death accident or overdose results in an earnest plea to God to give them one more chance. The ladies in recovery at Downtown Women's Center depend on us to help them get it right this time, to make their lives productive and help them restore their relationships with family and children. They are truly prodigal daughters.

Healthy relationships with families, friends, and God may be complicated at times. Women of addiction are conflicted between *I love you* and *I hate you*. They often lean on our Recovery Program, their case managers, and sisters in sobriety as their family until their real family bonds are healed. We accept women where they are with unconditional love, nurturing them back to mental, physical, and spiritual health. We are saving lives, giving children their mothers back, and restoring daughters to their families.

There is no adequate way to thank everyone who has contributed to the success of the hundreds of women and children who have passed through the doors of Downtown Women's Center. To those women and children we've not yet met, just know your lives will be changed for the better because of the people who love you before they even know who you are. Don't be afraid—just come.

Our Downtown Women's Center heroes include case managers who save lives; counselors who bless hearts and minds; volunteers who daily give time, talent, and treasure to complete strangers; and spiritual coach and one of the primary authors of this book, Sharon Miner, who fosters a love of God, sometimes for the first time, in our ladies in recovery. Thank you, Sharon, for sharing your wisdom and wonderful sense of humor with us all. We are so grateful!

Homelessness and addiction are color-blind and impact all cultures and socioeconomic levels. When women come to Downtown Women's Center to work our Recovery Program, many tell us, "Thank you for loving me before I could love myself." Many have said we saved their lives. The work of Downtown Women's Center is truly a ministry. We work for the Lord!

—Diann Gilmore, Executive Director
Downtown Women's Center

Redeemed! My brokenness was a choice.
I choose forgiveness for myself and for
others. Everyone is redeemable.
—DWC graduate

JANUARY

I am insecure.

I started my drinking career when I was only six years old. It was almost a given that I would become addicted, for every adult in my life had a bottle in their hands. I found Alateen at the age of fifteen after my stepdad, in a drunken stupor, smashed my head through a wall and had to face his own consequences of seeking recovery or else. His only punishment outside of probation was ninety meetings in ninety days. What injustice; I wasn't a fan of anonymous rooms. To forget about the family with whom I was forced to live, I snorted cocaine, smoked pot, and drank.

I eventually learned that drinking and drugging was not a good way to live out my life, so I went to PARC (Panhandle Alcohol Recovery Center) at the old air force base. I stayed in their program for twenty-eight days, stayed clean for approximately two weeks, then finally gave into temptation and was off to the races again. The fuel that kept my flame of addiction alive was the insecurity of my marriage, who I was, and what I stood for.

Sure, I wanted recovery. It was something I longed for, but it seemed so far out of reach. I have been gracing the doors of anonymous rooms for well over forty-two years. At one point, I had managed to rack up six years of sobriety, until the man I was attached to at the hip in the most toxic codependent relationship I have ever been privy to tried to kill me. I used my near-death experience and the fact that my child offered me a pipe as an excuse to make for the hills.

After years of being in a stupor, I lost my job, lost my identity, and decided it might be best if I just ended my life. I spoke to a counselor at TPC (Texas Panhandle Center of Behavioral Health) and told her I had no reason left to live. She met me at my mom's house, instructed me to unload all my work knives into the house, and then followed me inside. She then committed me to the Pavilion Mental Hospital. I did my time there, then relapsed a week after my discharge.

In 2015, I was busted for possession of meth, bonded out by my dear mother, and then went right back into the lifestyle I had grown accustomed to. I failed every urinalysis administered to me for jobs and probation. My probation officer gave me two weeks to find a rehab near my mother. I contacted Haven House and got on the waiting list. My phone rang two and a half weeks later, in the middle of an AA meeting, and I answered without thinking. "Are you ready?" was the question posed to me on the other end of the line. I couldn't quite recall setting up a date with anyone (I was prostituting at the time), so I got incredibly paranoid, wondering who was calling me. When she said she was from Haven House, I just began to cry with relief.

"Is this what you want?" she asked.

"If I don't get sober, I'll be dead," was my reply.

I went the next day and checked in, washed my clothes, signed all my paperwork, and slept like a baby. For the first six months, I attended ARAD (Amarillo Recovery from Drugs and Alcohol). I talked myself into believing that once I finished their program, I could go back to doing what I was doing all along. The Downtown Women's Center had a different plan for me. Once I completed ARAD, I was sent through drug court and subjected to three UAs a week. Meeting their requirements and completing their services would allow me to continue my walk.

I kept praying every day for God to help me feel better. I received an answer to my prayers and awoke one morning with a new attitude, a new lease on life, and what seemed to be a new physical body. I instantly decided then and there to surrender to the Lord and the program. I was no longer doing what I wanted to do on my terms. I poured my heart and soul into working on my program. I spent three separate weekends in jail for not following protocol in drug court to a T. I became grateful because I used that time to get closer to God and received a new perspective. I completed the DWC program in January 2018 and stayed in aftercare for one and a half years afterward. I have since found my own accommodations and am now living on my own—free.

I attend five to nine meetings a week, sponsor seven women in their programs of recovery, and volunteer my services every chance I get, on top of holding down three jobs. I owe my life and recovery to the Downtown Women's Center. I never knew this life existed for me.

I am restored!

New Strategies

We often write New Year's resolutions and the goals we set for the new year. There will be setbacks, disappointments, and the unexpected as the year unfolds. We cannot allow these challenges to derail us. He gives us grace, wisdom, provision, faith, guidance, joy, peace—everything we need for each day. He is the author of the dreams of our hearts.

> In this manner, therefore, pray: Our Father in heaven, Hallowed be Your name. Your kingdom come. Your will be done On earth as *it is* in heaven. Give us this day our daily bread. And forgive us our debts, As we forgive our debtors. And do not lead us into temptation, But deliver us from the evil one. For Yours is the kingdom and the power and the glory forever. Amen. (Matthew 6:9–13 NKJV)

Dream On

We think about our hopes, dreams, and plans as we approach the New Year. If we are honest, they are probably not new, just unfulfilled. The things that have stopped us in the past are still challenges. There are three reasons why we may not accomplish the desires of our hearts: we think the dream is too big, we don't seek wisdom, and we don't commit to the Lord.

Don't let another day go by without stepping into all that God has for you. Trust the Lord with the desires of your heart. He is faithful.

> Entrust your works to the LORD, and your plans will succeed. (Proverbs 16:3 NABRE)

I Declare

This is the time of year for goal-setting, New Year's resolutions, and ambitious plans. Sometimes we accomplish these, and sometimes we don't.

As you think about your hopes and dreams for the future, submit everything to the Lord. This is the right time to make a declaration to the One who will bring them to life.

> This I declare about the Lord: He alone is my refuge, my place of safety; he is my God, and I trust him. (Psalm 91:2 NLT)

Yesterday, Today, and Forever

Challenges come into our lives more often than we may want—sometimes expected, sometimes not. If Jesus Christ is our foundation, our everyday routines may be different, but our place with God is always solid. He is faithful. We will come through our challenges, maybe with a few edges knocked off but with a stronger and more solid faith than before.

Ask the Holy Spirit to be with you and your faith as you pray. Your prayer life is ongoing.

> Jesus Christ is the same yesterday and today and forever.
> (Hebrews 13:8 NIV)

January 5

What Are You Carrying?

Do you ever find yourself thinking about something, and before you know it, you are down the rabbit hole of worry? This path can lead to anxiety, fear, sleepless nights, and illness. God did not create you to carry such a burden. Remember that Jesus is always there, and He wants to carry every burden you have. As you pray, practice placing your cares with the Lord, trusting His care.

> Therefore, humble yourselves under the mighty hand of God, that He may exalt you in due time, casting all your care upon Him, for He cares for you. (1 Peter 5:6–7 NKJV)

What Do You Need?

When we consider our needs, they may be physical, emotional, or spiritual. The Word of God says He will supply all of our needs.

More importantly, don't forget to ask God's peace, patience, kindness, love, and faithfulness. In this way, you will have an abundance of faith and gifts to share with others. As you pray, open yourself to God's truths. Tell others. Believe together.

> And my God shall supply all your need according to His riches in glory by Christ Jesus. (Philippians 4:19 NKJV)

The Wait

Waiting on the Lord is not like waiting for the bus. It is a call to action. It is a call to believing God is going to move in every area of your life. It is a call to believing that His promises are true. As you wait, be still, and feel the presence of God. In prayer, ask the Holy Spirit to teach you to trust and have faith while waiting on the Lord.

> But those who wait on the Lord Shall renew their strength;
> They shall mount up with wings like eagles. They shall
> run and not be weary, they shall walk and not faint.
> (Isaiah 40:31 NKJV)

Now Faith Is

Our faith is determined by the trust we have now. Have we considered that God is showing us what is most important? Maybe He wants us to rearrange our personal and professional lives. God is up to something good. He is always moving us forward.

Have faith and hope in your future days. By doing so, the Holy Spirit will strengthen your faith.

> Now faith is the substance of things hoped for, the evidence of things not seen. (Hebrews 11:1 NKJV)

January 9

Keep Praising

Praise is more than a song. Praise is being thankful that God is the King of us all. You can sing and shout out your praises. You can praise Him through your tears. You will understand more through the practice of praising Him. As you lift up your heart and your prayers to the Lord, do so with song or writing in your journal. Let everything in you and all you know praise the Lord.

> God has gone up with a shout, The Lord with the sound of a trumpet. Sing praises to God, sing praises! Sing praises to our King, sing praises! For God is the King of all the earth; Sing praises with understanding. (Psalm 47:5–7 NKJV)

The Best Thing We Can Do

When things seem out of control, we may feel helpless. We believe there is nothing we can do. Whether in good times or challenging times, we can increase the power of our prayers. God has made us a promise that when we pray and seek His truth, He will hear our words and know our hearts.

In prayer, turn your face to the Lord, trusting that God will do His part. He will.

> If My people who are called by My name will humble themselves, and pray and seek My face, and turn from their wicked ways, then I will hear from heaven, and will forgive their sin and heal their land. (2 Chronicles 7:14 NKJV

The Search

Have you ever lost something that is precious to you? You might have been worried about your search, only to realize that what you were looking for wasn't that important. God promises when you search for Him with all your heart, you will find Him. As you pray, believe in that small still voice as you continue searching for the only Truth that promises to be found.

> Then you will call upon Me and go and pray to Me, and I will listen to you. And you will seek Me and find Me, when you search for Me with all your heart. (Jeremiah 29:12–13 NKJV)

Pray for Patience

Now is the time to live our faith fully and pray for patience.

Remain joyful, but don't deny your fears. Take each to the Lord. His promise of patience will strengthen both you and those close to you. His power will guide you through your challenges to a place of peace and acceptance.

> My brethren, count it all joy when you fall into various trials, knowing that the testing of your faith produces patience. But let patience have its perfect work, that you may be perfect and complete, lacking nothing. (James 1:2–4 NKJV)

January 13

Love Doesn't Know Distance

Our love for family and friends who live in different locations does not lessen because of distance. Our love for them remains powerful and strong. Christ lives in us; His love joins us together. God does not "socially distance" from us.

Pray, knowing time and distance will not separate you from the love that Christ has given you for family and friends.

> For I am persuaded that neither death nor life, nor angels nor principalities nor powers, nor things present nor things to come, nor height nor depth, nor any other created thing, shall be able to separate us from the love of God which is in Christ Jesus our Lord. (Romans 8:38–39 NKJV)

Light It Up

The Word of God shows us our next steps and gives us direction. Even when we don't see the path, by the power of the Holy Spirit, God illuminates our spirits and guides us into all truth. The path may not always be known to us, but light always dispels the dark.

Shine a light on your path by immersing yourself in the Word of God. He will share His light with you.

> Your word is a lamp to my feet And a light to my path.
> (Psalm 119:105 NKJV)

January 15

Living in Overflow

There is nothing keeping us from living our abundant lives. When we have Jesus as our source, we have eternal life.

No fear can take away your future. An abundant life means you are living from the love, joy, peace, grace, and mercy that comes naturally from your relationship with Jesus.

> The thief does not come except to steal, and to kill, and to destroy. I have come that they may have life, and that they may have it more abundantly. (John 10:10 NKJV)

Emmanuel

What a blessing it is to know that God is with us wherever we go. Do we realize He is also with us when we are still? Embracing His presence is what gives us strength and courage to endure.

Take time to acknowledge His presence by saying out loud, "God, you are with me," and let Him be your comfort.

> Have I not commanded you? Be strong and of good courage; do not be afraid, nor be dismayed, for the Lord your God is with you wherever you go. (Joshua 1:9 NKJV)

The Goodness of God

God is powerful, and He uses His power to help us overcome! The Spirit of the living God dwells in us, and we have everything we may need. He has called us by name. He invites us to know and see the good works of the Lord.

Rest and be still in the goodness of God.

> Everything we could ever need for life and godliness has already been deposited in us by his divine power. For all this was lavished upon us through the rich experience of knowing him who has called us by name and invited us to come to him through a glorious manifestation of his goodness. (2 Peter 1:3 TPT)

It's Not Just a Symbol

When Jesus gave up His spirit on the cross, we received life. At that moment, God gave us freedom to believe, freedom to know we are enough and to live with faith in our daily world of work, family, and friends. The cross isn't just a symbol. It is our true and everlasting hope.

> Looking unto Jesus, the author and finisher of our faith, who for the joy that was set before Him endured the cross, despising the shame, and has sat down at the right hand of the throne of God. (Hebrews 12:2 NKJV)

January 19

Imagine

Imagine you had walked with Jesus. You were there when He was laid in the tomb. Imagine the thoughts that would have gone through your mind and the hopelessness you might have felt then.

Jesus is alive among us now. His message is alive—that he has a place for us and that we are not lost. His promises are real and made alive through our daily walks of faith.

Just imagine.

> For I know that my Redeemer lives, And He shall stand
> at last on the earth. (Job 19:25 NKJV)

Rejoice

Rejoice and be glad, for Jesus is alive. You have resurrection power because the same spiritual power that raised Christ from the dead is alive in you. Live your life knowing that Jesus is the way, the truth, and the life.

> But if the Spirit of Him who raised Jesus from the dead dwells in you, He who raised Christ from the dead will also give life to your mortal bodies through His Spirit who dwells in you. (Romans 8:11 NKJV)

January 21

Let's Go Fishing

It's not necessarily a bad thing that the disciples went fishing again after they met the risen Savior. After all, some of them had first met Jesus by the sea. It might have given them a sense of comfort.

It's time to live out your faith in real ways now, showing others that to know His way is the comfort way, the true way.

> And He said to them, "Cast the net on the right side of the boat, and you will find some." So they cast, and now they were not able to draw it in because of the multitude of fish. (John 21:6 NKJV)

It's a New Thing

Sometimes we have to let go of our pasts so we can know our futures. A spiritual wilderness also can be a place of healing. A spiritual desert can be flushed with living water.

See with spiritual eyes, whether wilderness or desert, mountaintop or valley. God is with you in all these places.

> Do not remember the former things, Nor consider the things of old. Behold, I will do a new thing, Now it shall spring forth; Shall you not know it? I will even make a road in the wilderness And rivers in the desert. (Isaiah 43:18–19 NKJV)

Unconditional Gifts

Every miracle, every blessing, every good thing that has happened in our lives is of the Lord. He blesses from His own heart in true ways. His gifts are unconditional. We don't have to be anything except who we are. His blessings are freely given.

Now is the right time for you to practice receiving. Receiving is harder sometimes than giving—another learning moment, another blessing.

> Every good gift and every perfect gift is from above, coming down from the Father of lights, with whom there is no variation or shadow due to change. (James 1:17 ESV)

Send It Out

Every time we read the Bible, we have an encounter with the living God, the Creator of heaven and earth. His Word never grows old. His Word is life-giving and always true. When we listen, read, or speak the Word of God, His purpose is real to us.

Dance with God's Word, and let His rhythm move you to the place He has prepared for you.

> "It is the same with My word. I send it out, and it always produces fruit. It will accomplish all I want it to, and it will prosper everywhere I send it." (Isaiah 55:11 NLT)

The One Thing

When we go to God's house in prayer, He opens His door and greets us with His open love. A beautiful exchange takes place in this heavenly hello, where we are made whole. Prayer may change our situation, but more importantly, it changes us. Dwelling in God's house through prayer gives us peace and courage.

Be the house guest who never leaves.

> Here's the one thing I crave from Yahweh, the one thing I seek above all else: I want to live with him every moment in his house, beholding the marvelous beauty of Yahweh, filled with awe, delighting in his glory and grace. I want to contemplate in his temple. (Psalm 27:4 TPT)

Be a Reflection

Mornings bring the reality of looking in the mirror and deciding all we see. What we see is not as pure as what God sees. He sees the unique splendor and awe of a special people He has created in His image. Our beliefs about God are reflected in our kindness with others. Sometimes we forget to be kind to ourselves.

Accept the Lord's free gift of your unique self, and live as God's magnificent creation.

> So God created man in His own image; in the image of
> God He created him; male and female He created them.
> (Genesis 1:27 NKJV)

January 27

It's a Promise

God's plan for our lives has not changed. His desire to see us grow, spiritually and physically, is still God's plan for us. Jesus is the Master Builder, and what He builds will not go away or be destroyed.

As you invest your time with the Lord, you will best know the design He has for your future.

> "For I know the plans I have for you," says the Lord.
> "They are plans for good and not for disaster, to give you
> a future and a hope." (Jeremiah 29:11 NLT)

We Will Be Better

Our faith is stronger as God brings us through each challenge. It is His mission to prepare us for our tomorrows. Whatever we are going through will not last forever. God is faithful. He will lead the way. Sometimes, we have a harder time being a follower than a leader.

Trust the Lord as the true leader. You will not be disappointed.

> And then, after your brief suffering, the God of all loving grace, who has called you to share in his eternal glory in Christ, will personally and powerfully restore you and make you stronger than ever. Yes, he will set you firmly in place and build you up. And he has all the power needed to do this—forever! Amen. (1 Peter 5:10–11 TPT)

It's Just a Decision

We are faced daily with decisions that make up the flow of our days. It is up to us, however, to be responsible for the choices we make. It is our decision to love God with all our hearts and all our souls. It is our decision to love our neighbors as ourselves. As we make these decisions daily, we will know and can trust the will of God for our lives.

> Jesus answered him, "The first of all the commandments is: 'Hear, O Israel, the LORD our God, the LORD is one. And you shall love the LORD your God with all your heart, with all your soul, with all your mind, and with all your strength.' This *is* the first commandment. And the second, like *it, is* this: 'You shall love your neighbor as yourself.' There is no other commandment greater than these." (Mark 12:29–31 NKJV)

Sow It

A natural response to physical activity is feeling tired. Weariness can also be a condition of the heart. Protecting our hearts is a responsibility the Lord desires us to do. We plant good seed in our hearts when we pay attention to what we see, what we hear, what we speak. This is how we gain our spiritual strength and our hope. This is how we know our spiritual power is used for the goodness of others.

> And don't allow yourselves to be weary in planting good seeds, for the season of reaping the wonderful harvest you've planted is coming! (Galatians 6:9 TPT)

January 31

Are You Convinced?

Life is a tapestry of events woven together to create who we are. God stitches the good and bad events in our lives, using the thread of His love. In this way, He reveals His wonderful purpose for each of us. Our love of God allows us to see He is the curator and keeper of the days of our lives. We are His tapestry.

> So we are convinced that every detail of our lives is continually woven together for good, for we are his lovers who have been called to fulfill his designed purpose. (Romans 8:28 TPT)

I am flawed but still loved by God.
—volunteer, DWC Ladies Auxiliary

FEBRUARY

I am stuck in toxic relationships.

Divine intervention: "a miracle or act of God that causes something good to happen or stops something bad from happening" (https://www.yourdictionary.com/divine-intervention).

An example could be someone awakening after several years in a coma. I most definitely was in a drug-induced coma, metaphorically speaking, for most of my adult life.

I started drinking at the age of fifteen. I soon found myself in a toxic relationship that resulted in a pregnancy at age seventeen. We stayed together for almost seven years. Because of our codependent nature and reliance on selfish behaviors, taking drugs seemed an easy answer to a bigger problem that we were not yet ready to face.

We eventually parted ways, and soon after, I met yet another man. We moved in together, and I soon became pregnant once again—only this relationship was ten times more toxic than the last, and my addictions were in full swing.

I had never learned healthy coping skills; therefore, I turned to drugs and alcohol every time life took a left turn. I would have seasons of clarity, followed by efforts to get my life together, one of which was to further my education at Amarillo College. I got a DWI and totaled my car in my last semester at Amarillo College. Thankfully, my children were not in the vehicle. This DWI would be the first of many encounters with the law. I graduated from Amarillo College in 2012 with my associate's degree in criminal justice, and soon, life took a nosedive. I was more lost than ever, trying to get out of another long toxic relationship. Because of a domestic violence case, Child Protective Services had removed my boys, and I finally had gotten custody of them, but I still didn't know how to be a healthy and responsible mother. Eventually, I agreed to have my first son's dad and his family care for him. And through many struggles, I finally left my relationship, but in doing that, I had to leave my second son behind with his father.

I became detached from reality and began living with a drug dealer. I was completely cut off from what I used to know. Here I was, with a college degree, yet living a life of crime, heavily addicted to drugs. I didn't talk to my family or children for almost four years. I always ran away from the one thing I wanted the most because of the daily shame that tore through my soul. During that time, I was on the news because of drug raids, and the shame continued to suffocate me.

God's grace dismissed the charges, but I continued down a dark road, half the time living with a drug dealer and the other half homeless because my paranoia would get the best of me. Along the way, I experienced many losses, but mostly I lost my sense of value and worth. In October 2017, I found a new bottom, resulting in five felonies that would not be dismissed this time. I signed up for five years of probation and stayed sober for a few months. I found yet another man and a new town to keep me sober. This relationship resulted in another relapse and put me in another bad situation. I found myself back in jail on new charges. No matter how much I ran, I always found myself waiting for me at the new location. This time I just knew I was going to prison. The hardest part of that was finding out I was expecting another baby. Wholly crushed and desperate for a new life, I began looking to God for guidance, praying every day for His will to be done so that I might find freedom from the insanity of this addiction that was killing me softly. I desperately wanted to be a mother again and to find peace.

When I was released from jail, it was a pure miracle from God. I knew this was another chance, and I was not going back this time. I vowed to be a good mother to my boys and my new baby on the way. Two days after being released from jail, I moved into Haven House at the Downtown Women's Center. It was a starting point for my new life. I had been through many other rehabs during my wandering days, but I always had reservations that I would use again. It must not have been the right timing or tools for me to successfully rebuild my life.

With just the clothes on my back, I began my new life at DWC. They furnished everything I needed, including refreshment for my broken and empty soul. Diann Gilmore, Brittany Jenkins, and Jenni Mays were my mentors and began loving me in ways I had never experienced before. Three months into my stay at Haven House, my second son was returned to me by his father. That's when I moved into the Abba House.

God winked at me and reminded me that He was always with me and that I was worthy of a good life. My son was also very broken from our life of addiction. DWC helped him find healing for his wounds as well. In October 2018, I gave birth to an eight-pound three-ounce healthy baby boy. Today, I get to be a mom to all three of my boys. In February 2019, I began working at Thrift City, DWC's thrift store. There, I learned how to care for myself and my family financially. In April 2019, I moved up another level, and the Downtown Women's Center offered me my very own beautiful two-bedroom, two-bath apartment. I give all credit to God for placing His hands on my life and using DWC to rebuild my life in a joyous and successful way. DWC has helped me overcome obstacles that I thought I would never get through. Not only have I gotten through them, but I have learned how to live life without men, without drugs, and without alcohol. For that, my boys and I are truly grateful. I am a full-time student at West Texas A&M University and work part-time at the college. The chapters of my story continue to get more enriched with love and success—all because of the helping hands at Downtown Women's Center.

I am a mighty woman of God!

February 1

Picture-Perfect Peace

Often, we search for peace in places of comfort, only to find a false peace. Careers, social gatherings, and other people become our escape where we find temporary solace. It takes faith and courage to believe we can remain in perfect peace. The peace that Jesus offers is not without challenges. He promises we can have and know this peace—the kind of peace that goes beyond the challenges that seem overwhelming. Yes, these too.

> I leave the gift of peace with you—my peace. Not the kind of fragile peace given by the world, but my perfect peace. Don't yield to fear or be troubled in your hearts—instead, be courageous! (John 14:27 TPT)

Remember When

Reminiscing about special vacations and holidays with family and friends brings us warm and pleasant feelings. It makes us happy and joyful when we take time to remember the miracles and wonders that God has given us. All of these—and more—add to our thankfulness. Our faith grows stronger as we remember that He delivered us once, and He will do it again. We will never be far from the goodness of God.

> Yet I could never forget all your miracles, my God, as I remember all your wonders of old. (Psalm 77:11 TPT)

February 3

The Comforter

God has given us the power to minister hope and comfort to others in times of trouble. He has poured out hope and comfort to us. If we search our hearts, we will find the gift of encouragement. Deciding to keep it or give it away is not a choice we have to make. We receive it in order to give it away.

Let the Comforter comfort you, as you comfort others, whether near or far.

> He comforts us in all our troubles so that we can comfort others. When they are troubled, we will be able to give them the same comfort God has given us. (2 Corinthians 1:4 NLT)

What Are You Saying?

Every day, we shape our world by what we say. The words we speak and the tone of our voices determine our future. Many conflicts have happened because a negative word was spoken. In the same way, many lives have been restored because good and true words were spoken.

Listen to the words you say and the tone you use. You just might be someone's only lifeline to their tomorrow.

> Death and life *are* in the power of the tongue, And those who love it will eat its fruit. (Proverbs 18:21 NKJV)

Hear the Sound

The sound of thunder in a storm lets us know God is speaking. When we gaze at the beauty of a rainbow after the storm, His voice becomes a brilliant light. When we smell the freshness of the rain and feel the warmth of the sun, we know the power of His voice. This gives us the assurance that God is with us. The force and goodness of His voice is more powerful than any storm.

> The voice of the Lord echoes through the skies and seas. The Glory-God reigns as he thunders in the clouds. So powerful is his voice, so brilliant and bright—how majestic as he thunders over the great waters! (Psalm 29:3–4 TPT)

We Can't Help but Win

In the valley of our challenges, we usually turn to face them or turn away and surrender to our fears. By His love, we are encouraged to overcome and to climb out of our valleys, however deep each may seem. We overcome by knowing our true identities are in Christ. His continuing love will take us from the valleys to the mountaintops, where we truly belong and live in Him.

> Yet in all these things we are more than conquerors through Him who loved us. (Romans 8:37 NKJV)

Come Together

Collectively, we are a people who represent Jesus Christ on this earth. Our individual lives, when woven together, create an atmosphere that encourages others to want to be a part of the great things the Lord is doing. When we have common goals, we have the opportunity to show the character of God to others in faith and with joy.

> How truly wonderful and delightful it is to see brothers and sisters living together in sweet unity! (Psalm 133:1 TPT)

Let It Be Done

Doubt can lead to a crisis of faith. When we forget that God is bigger than any of our mountains, we can fall into uncertainty. When we keep our faith in God, we see Him move in our lives.

When the challenges you face seem too big for you, and doubt rises up, remember that your faith in God will be with you today and tomorrow. You are not alone. God's presence is with you, twenty-four/seven.

> So Jesus answered and said to them, "Have faith in God. For assuredly, I say to you, whoever says to this mountain, 'Be removed and be cast into the sea,' and does not doubt in his heart, but believes that those things he says will be done, he will have whatever he says." (Mark 11:22–23 NKJV)

Move with Compassion

Compassion is a word we don't regularly use. Compassion comes with responsibility. When our hearts are filled with compassion, something powerful happens. It compels us to act out of the greater love we have been given. As we act from that love, the love of Christ shines forth on all of us. Compassion is a love action.

> And Jesus, when He came out, saw a great multitude and was moved with compassion for them, because they were like sheep not having a shepherd. So He began to teach them many things. (Mark 6:34 NKJV)

Stay In!

Safety is a priority, but we give little thought to it. It's just an assumption that most of us are able to make. Places where we feel safest are different for all of us. Staying in and acknowledging the presence of the Lord is our true safe place.

When you find yourself getting lost in the storms of daily life, find your place to stand and be safe. Remember the power in the very name of Jesus to keep you safe.

> The name of the LORD *is* a strong tower; The righteous
> run to it and are safe. (Proverbs 18:10 NKJV)

Live

Fully knowing that Christ lives in us is a burst of energy, full of color and power. To be alive in Christ, we are transformed, and living by faith is how we do life best.

Make a decision to live daily in the joy and peace that comes with knowing the power and color of the Son of the living God.

> I have been crucified with Christ; it is no longer I who live, but Christ lives in me; and the *life* which I now live in the flesh I live by faith in the Son of God, who loved me and gave Himself for me. (Galatians 2:20 NKJV)

The Truth

Sometimes it is hard to recognize the truth because it is not shown to us in a way that matches how we view the world. The struggle is not about what we see and hear. The struggle is often about how we shape our faith. We are helped as we clear space in our lives and in our faith to move from untruth to truth.

> Then Jesus said to those Jews who believed Him, "If you abide in My word, you are My disciples indeed. And you shall know the truth, and the truth shall make you free." (John 8:31–32 NKJV)

February 13

Power in Weakness

External events can create pressure to change our situations. Dwelling on events we don't control can make us uncertain and unsure of what to do first. When we meditate on His grace and His peace, however, we find our sufficiency. His grace is enough and gives us the power and the wisdom to thrive.

> But he answered me, "My grace is always more than enough for you, and my power finds its full expression through your weakness." So I will celebrate my weaknesses, for when I'm weak I sense more deeply the mighty power of Christ living in me. (2 Corinthians 12:9 TPT)

Love Is a Choice

Love is a feeling, a choice, and a commitment. If we are waiting for a feeling before we love others, we should take a look at Jesus. He came to earth with love for us all. Throughout His thirty-three years of life and ministry, He demonstrated unconditional love through His actions and, ultimately, by dying on the cross.

Pray that your love for others will be a reflection of Jesus's unending and complete love for you!

> Love is patient and kind. Love is not jealous or boastful or proud or rude. It does not demand its own way. It is not irritable, and it keeps no record of being wronged. It does not rejoice about injustice but rejoices whenever the truth wins out. Love never gives up, never loses faith, is always hopeful, and endures through every circumstance. (1 Corinthians 13:4–7 NLT)

February 15

The Secret Place

Our hearts are often hidden by our reactions to a situation or event. Our responses shout out what we believe, but when we are hidden in Christ, the hidden becomes seen by all.

Allow the Father to minister to your spirit and heal your heart. Stand with Him, and be amazed by the light that now shines outward from you.

> For there is nothing hidden that will not become visible, and nothing secret that will not be known and come to light. (Luke 8:17 NABRE)

Get Quiet

Prayer can be a time of both asking and receiving. More importantly, prayer can speak to us about giving back in bigger ways than we ever imagined.

Don't limit your prayers to what God might do for you. Pray, from all you know, to know more about the goodness and the blessings of God. Prayer changes those around you. Prayer changes you.

> But when you pray, go into your room, close the door and pray to your Father, who is unseen. Then your Father, who sees what is done in secret, will reward you. (Matthew 6:6 NIV)

February 17

What Would Jesus Do (WWJD)?

How do you react when you are faced with a big challenge? Do you ask yourself what to do, or do you ask which decisions would Jesus make in this situation? In order to answer, you must know the character and nature of God, revealed through His Son.

When we remain in Christ, we figure out the answers to the challenges we face. There is a God response to every situation.

> For who has ever intimately known the mind of the Lord Yahweh well enough to become his counselor? Christ has, and we possess Christ's perceptions. (1 Corinthians 2:16 TPT)

Hold On

A promise from God is always true. We cannot forget that His truth greets us each morning. He knows all about our challenges, our weaknesses, our strengths.

Hold tightly and stay close to your true hope, which is found in Jesus. He will be with you in your mornings and your nights.

> So now wrap your heart tightly around the hope that lives within us, knowing that God always keeps his promises! (Hebrews 10:23 TPT)

February 19

Reality Check

Just as our physical bodies need food, our spirits must be fed as well. What we touch, taste, hear, and see stimulates our minds and teaches us what we think. When we renew our minds to the Word of God, our spirits become sensitive to the will of God. It is our joy, then, to allow God's will to shape and let us know God's reality.

> Do not be conformed to this age, but be transformed by the renewing of your mind, so that you may discern what is the good, pleasing, and perfect will of God. (Romans 12:2 CSB)

Break Free

There is a permanent freedom that cannot be limited by external forces. We are free from worry, anxiety, and failure because the Son released us from discouragement and raised us up to know and proclaim the hope and goodness of the Lord. We stay free as we stay faithful to the Lord in prayer and in service to others.

> So if the Son sets you free, you will be free indeed. (John 8:36 NIV)

Treasure Hunt

God loves us as we look to Him, and as we do, we gain a deeper understanding of His grace and goodness. We can find His goodness in the smallest of details in our daily lives. If we ask and seek the Lord, He will show us His truth. We will live our lives from knowing and trusting His truths.

> Those who love me I also love, and those who seek me find me. (Proverbs 8:17 NABRE)

I Have a Plan

It takes discipline to trust that God will still be there when we work through our challenges. Building our trust in God leads us to constant conversation with God. By doing so, we develop our desire and willingness to submit everything we do and have to the Lord.

Trust in God daily, and make His priority your priority.

> In all your ways be mindful of him, and he will make straight your paths. (Proverbs 3:6 NABRE)

February 23

The Calm after the Storm

There is calm after a storm, creating peace in ways we never thought possible. This peace, the Lord's peace, surpasses all we understand. In this time of recovery, we find our spiritual restoration and the purpose God has for us upon the earth.

Look for the rainbow at the end of every storm. This is where you will find your hope.

> But may the God of all grace, who called us to His eternal glory by Christ Jesus, after you have suffered a while, perfect, establish, strengthen, and settle *you*. To Him *be* the glory and the dominion forever and ever. Amen. (1 Peter 5:10–11 NKJV)

Beyond Blessings

Over our lives, we are blessed with many possessions. We know material things do not define our worth to God. His blessings go beyond all we see and know. There is a generous spirit behind the blessings we receive. Each shows us the grace and goodness of the Lord. His favor will bless us forever.

> True enrichment comes from the blessing of the Lord, with rest and contentment in knowing that it all comes from him. (Proverbs 10:22 TPT)

No Limits

Where do we go when we need answers? Sometimes, we rely on our own knowledge, search the internet, or ask a friend. These sources are limited in the information they provide. We are not always able to know whether these answers can be trusted.

Wisdom from God can be trusted and is always available to you. There is no other source truer or longer lasting. Pray for this trusted wisdom. You will not be disappointed.

> If any of you lacks wisdom, let him ask of God, who gives
> to all liberally and without reproach, and it will be given
> to him. (James 1:5 NKJV)

Finding Grace

When our eyes and hearts are focused on God's truth, grace and mercy grow within us and strengthen our spirits. No matter what we have done, are doing, or will do, we will enter into the presence of God, knowing that His grace will protect us. In a time when there are more questions than answers, God's wisdom will be our source of what is true and trustworthy.

> Let us then approach God's throne of grace with confidence, so that we may receive mercy and find grace to help us in our time of need. (Hebrews 4:16 NIV)

Humble State of Mind

Think of a time when you needed help, but it was not in your nature to ask.

When we humble ourselves to the Lord, we find our true help. We don't always know everything. When our minds and hearts are open to receive the truth, God will provide all we need and want to know.

> Keep showing the humble your path, and lead them into the best decision. Bring revelation-light that trains them in the truth. (Psalm 25:9 TPT)

Special Delivery

Have you ever been in fear of something you think is going to happen?

If we become locked into that mindset of worry, we wander away from our trust in the Lord. If we continue to trust in the Lord, fear and worry cannot find a home in our spirits. The Word of God promises to deliver us from our fears, and this is true.

> For I am the LORD, your God, who grasp your right hand;
> It is I who say to you, Do not fear, I will help you. (Isaiah 41:13 NABRE)

I am set free of the drug addiction that
turned me into somebody I never thought
in a million years I would be.

—DWC employee

MARCH

I am abused.

Growing up in a small town didn't leave much to the imagination for an inquisitive young girl. I knew I had a problem with alcohol when I sought out our small-town recreation center for teens as a place to drink or get high. I was one of eight surviving children in my large Catholic family. I knew I was loved, but I was never shown love. We took on the chores, such as cleaning, ironing, cooking, babysitting, hanging clothes out on the line, and so forth. Any time I was able to get away from the house, my first instinct was to run as far away as I could, just to remove myself from the adult responsibilities that were placed on me at a young age.

I was athletic, so I started using my running to be beneficial to myself and my school, and I excelled in track and field. I loved school and made good grades, but I wasn't allowed to study at home because there was too much work to do. My mom believed that all my schooling could be done at school. She ran our home like a drill sergeant.

My parents were hardworking and sacrificed so much to provide for their family. Dad was a gifted musician, and that was his therapy. Mom devoted all her time to her family and her home. They had been married sixty-seven years when Dad passed, and Mom followed him precisely one year, one day, and one hour later.

I married at the age of nineteen. At the age of twenty, I had my firstborn, and one year and one day later, my second child was born. My husband and I drank together, and it was more than explosive in our home. I still wear the scars of those dark days. I started smoking pot because we wouldn't fight as much when we were high. Eleven years went by while we stayed in torment. I was physically and mentally abused. I saw no way out and felt like I needed to stay because of my sons. I realize now that was the worst mistake I could have made. My adult sons still suffer from the decisions made by their addicted parents.

We did what most families did. We hid in plain sight; we graced the doors of our church every Sunday. Due to the close relationship between our pastor and our families, I could not talk to him. I desperately wanted to talk about what was happening in our home to someone. I earnestly waited for the right opportunity, which came in the form of a visiting minister. I poured my heart out to him, and he gave me the answer I so desperately sought.

"God did not mean for you to live life that way. He wants harmony and peace in a marriage."

I finally gathered my strength and moved on from my crumbling marriage. I played the blame game daily. It was always everyone else's fault. I didn't even give myself a chance to heal before getting into a new relationship. My sons were twelve and eleven, and we added two more sons and a stepson. At the beginning of our eighteen-year marriage, we moved to a ranch outside town. We didn't drink for several years. We all worked well together as a team. We managed our money well, went camping and fishing after big roofing jobs, and enjoyed one another's company. Life was incredible; there was peace, but we were still smoking pot daily.

We then moved to Montana to be close to his dad and family. We lived there for seven years. My husband didn't like keeping a job, so we struggled occasionally. I worked in Montana and had a good bit of money saved in my 401(k). We decided to move back to Texas and bought a house with our small savings. When we moved back to Texas, we started doing meth. I was terrified to be in the same room with my paranoid husband and wasn't even sure what was going on most of the time. My children saw a side of me as well that scared them. We ended up divorced. I used up all my money on drugs and alcohol and lost my car when I wrecked it and got a DWI. I was lost more days than I wasn't.

Potter County jail was the new reality. Once in, I was able to sober up and realize my fate. I was an alcoholic, drug-addicted mom of a son planning his wedding and buying a home. Feeling pretty helpless, I threw my hands up and said, "God, You say that You won't put more on me than I can handle. I am *there*! Please help me! I'll do whatever I have to." Then I cried myself to sleep. I couldn't afford to pay my fines and ticket, so I went back to jail to sit out my sentence. I did some major soul-searching while behind bars, and I realized what I was doing wasn't working.

My son came to pick me up when I got out of jail. I got on the phone to start making arrangements, not knowing who I was calling, but a sweet woman on the other end of the line asked me to come to the Haven. I reluctantly showed up, all the while rationalizing that I just needed to do this program for alcohol and meth, and once completed, I could go back to smoking my weed.

It wasn't long before the good seeds sown in me as a child—to always do things to the best of my ability—took center stage, and I committed myself entirely to the program—hook, line, and sinker. I have been clean and sober ever since October 11, 2003. Only God knew that He would bring me full circle back to the place that saved my life. I now work alongside the people who showed me the way to freedom, and I help others through this program at the Downtown Women's Center. He wants me to give back what was given to me. It is mind-boggling when I think about God's grace and how Jesus's healing restored my relationship with my sons and family.

I have since married an amazing man who loves me and treats me with the kindness of Christ. To have life and life abundant, one must submit to the recovery and redemption that the Lord offers us daily, if only we will receive. We all have choices to make, and recovery is one of the hardest but the most rewarding.

I am loved!

Silence Is Golden

It can be challenging to remain in silence. During our quiet and meditation time, there are sounds within our homes or the outside street. Silence is different when the home and street traffic quieten. We then experience the pureness of what silence can be.

Identify your quiet place in your home. Take a few minutes every day and allow the silence to be your teacher. Hear the voice of the Lord in the stillness.

> The LORD will fight for you; you have only to keep still.
> (Exodus 14:14 NABRE)

Stay Thirsty

All of humanity requires water to survive. Spiritually, it is the true living water that Jesus provides that leads us to live a life of balance and wholeness. Every drink of His living water feeds our hearts and gives us the spiritual energy to thrive.

> Jesus answered and said to her, "If you knew the gift of God, and who it is who says to you, 'Give Me a drink,' you would have asked Him, and He would have given you living water." (John 4:10 NKJV)

Guard Your Heart

Most of us have cared for young children, paying close attention to every physical move they make. We focus on protecting them and are constantly on the lookout to keep them safe.

Pay attention to the promises from God; He wants you to know. Guard your heart, and base your life and relationships on these. You will not be disappointed in the fulfillment of God's promises to keep you safe from harm.

> So above all, guard the affections of your heart, for they affect all that you are. Pay attention to the welfare of your innermost being, for from there flows the wellspring of life. (Proverbs 4:23 TPT)

March 4

Show Integrity

No good outcome comes from acting better than others. People are drawn to us or move away from us because of our behaviors and our values. Neighbors, family, or coworkers trust us or not, as we show ourselves for who and what we are. When we understand that we attract people through our integrity, then our hearts and minds are best prepared to receive and share the good news with those around us.

> In all things showing yourself *to be* a pattern of good works; in doctrine *showing* integrity, reverence, incorruptibility, sound speech that cannot be condemned, that one who is an opponent may be ashamed, having nothing evil to say of you. (Titus 2:7–8 NKJV)

Are You Curious?

In challenging times, we return to what is comfortable.

Do not fear the future. Get curious about God's blessings for you. Because they are from God, they will not go away or be hidden from you. Each will open your eyes and fill your heart with all that is possible.

> There the angel of the Lord appeared to him in flames of fire from within a bush. Moses saw that though the bush was on fire it did not burn up. So Moses thought, "I will go over and see this strange sight—why the bush does not burn up." (Exodus 3:2–3 NIV)

March 6

No Other gods before Him

We all have people and events in our lives that are important to us. There can be pleasure and excitement connected to these, even as temporary pleasures. When we worship the Lord, we are changed today and forever, placing God above everything in our lives.

Make a list of all that you place before God, and have no other gods before Him.

> For the Lord is great and greatly to be praised; He is to be feared above all gods. For all the gods of the peoples are idols, But the Lord made the heavens. (Psalm 96:4–5 NKJV)

Heal Your Spirit

If our physical bodies are injured, we seek treatment. When our spirits become bruised and even broken, we are not sure to whom or where to turn. It is during these unsure times that we humble ourselves by turning to the Lord. It is a bruised spirit, when healed, that can best show the richness of the Lord to others.

> The sacrifices of God *are* a broken spirit, A broken and a contrite heart—These, O God, You will not despise. (Psalm 51:17 NKJV)

March 8

Faith on Purpose

It is our responsibility to join the Lord in growing our faith. Every decision we make either adds to or diminishes our faith. This is why we include others in making faith decisions. In doing so, we are sharing the Lord. By broadening our faith, we deepen our faith and, hopefully, the faith of others.

> For this very reason, make every effort to supplement your faith with goodness, goodness with knowledge, knowledge with self-control, self-control with endurance, endurance with godliness, godliness with brotherly affection, and brotherly affection with love. (2 Peter 1:5–7 CSB)

Complete Me, Lord

Babies are born with everything they need for their early lives. They soon learn to talk, walk, and experience years of growth and learning. God's gifts of love, peace, and kindness with us and with others encourage us to understand and share the Lord with others. This is how we add to our lives and the lives of others.

> For I am confident of this very thing, that He who began
> a good work in you will perfect it until the day of Christ
> Jesus. (Philippians 1:6 NAB)

Do the Right Thing

Doing the right thing is a choice. Options for right or wrong are placed before us. We decide which direction we take, whether up or down, left or right. Our opinions can be faulty, but the wisdom of God is always right and just. We will be guided to what is good and right.

Just make a choice.

> Let us choose for ourselves what is right; Let us know among ourselves what is good. (Job 34:4 NIV)

Who Is Your Influence?

Most of us have someone we trust and allow into our lives. We know it is important that the people to whom we listen are speaking truth. We introduce those in whom we have faith to others. To know and share the truth of the Lord is a special blessing.

> But Ruth said, "Do not urge me to leave you or turn back from following you; for where you go, I will go, and where you lodge, I will lodge. Your people shall be my people, and your God, my God." (Ruth 1:16 NLT)

March 12

What's Past Is Prologue

Have you ever wanted to rewrite your past?

We can spend time reflecting on the past and telling ourselves that if we had only done things differently, our lives would be different. That might be true, but if we ask ourselves what we learned, we can use that information to have the best of future days. Our pasts are how God prepares us for our futures.

> Whatever is has already been, and what will be has been before; and God will call the past to account. (Ecclesiastes 3:15 NIV)

Terms and Conditions

Let's be honest. How many times have we actually read the terms and conditions that we sign to buy something or join a group? We click the I-accept button but generally have no idea what we agreed to. Having faith in God comes with terms and conditions that are called His promises. When we click the yes button to allow God to use us, we are signing for greater things than we ever imagined.

> Most assuredly, I say to you, he who believes in Me, the works that I do he will do also; and greater works than these he will do, because I go to My Father. (John 14:12 NKJV)

March 14

Just Do It

Do we really need to pray about things that God has told us to do? He has told us to love our neighbors, so just do it. He has told us to help the least of these, so just do it. He has told us not to judge others, so don't do that. He has told us to forgive, so just do it. There is a place for obedience in our lives of prayer and service to others.

> But Samuel replied: "Does the Lord delight in burnt offerings and sacrifices as much as in obeying the Lord? To obey is better than sacrifice, and to heed is better than the fat of rams." (1 Samuel 15:22 NIV)

What's Hiding in Your Heart?

The pain and hurt in our lives are often hidden within our hearts. The emotion of these issues can, at times, overwhelm us. We pray that the Lord will search our hearts and let all things hidden come to light. We pray this light will be used to make us better, more whole persons.

> There is nothing concealed that will not be disclosed, or hidden that will not be made known. (Luke 12:2 NIV)

Sharpen Your Tools

Most of us have tools in our homes for repairs. The more we use a tool, the more our knowledge and skill of that tool improves. Through practice, we learn to use our tools to build or repair. When it comes to the issues of life and faith, the Word of God becomes our tool. The Word of God will strengthen our hearts with His love. The world will notice.

> Keep on doing what you have learned and received and heard and seen in me. Then the God of peace will be with you. (Philippians 4:9 NABRE)

Let Us Focus

Sharing our faith and the events of God in our lives is amazing. If we become concerned with what people think of us, we will not get to God's intended next stage. The way we express our faith is matched to how we live our lives.

In faith, be consistent with your focus on the Lord.

> Then the woman of Samaria said to Him, "How is it that You, being a Jew, ask a drink from me, a Samaritan woman?" For Jews have no dealings with Samaritans. Jesus answered and said to her, "If you knew the gift of God, and who it is who says to you, 'Give Me a drink,' you would have asked Him, and He would have given you living water." (John 4:9–10 NKJV)

March 18

You Ain't Seen Nothing Yet

Believing and thinking something is not the same. What we believe is shown in our actions. What we think can sometimes be hidden from us. Believing in our future takes enormous courage when the valleys become mountains.

Give yourself permission to know and be pleased about the Lord's plan for your future.

> But as it is written: "Eye has not seen, nor ear heard, Nor have entered into the heart of man The things which God has prepared for those who love Him." (1 Corinthians 2:9 NKJV)

Use Your Voice

We use our voices every day. The sound, volume, and tone of our voices can make or break our connection with others. Whether we are talking to one person or a thousand, communication is everything. The words we speak may empower someone who is prepared and ready to go out and change the world.

> From the same mouth come blessing and cursing. This need not be so, my brothers. (James 3:10 NABRE)

Look Inside

Have you opened a door to a room and been surprised by who and what was there? Did you experience a fight-or-flight reaction? When God opens the door to your heart, don't hesitate when He shows you His truth. Say, "Welcome! Show me more. I have been waiting for you."

> Search me, O God, and know my heart; Try me, and know my anxieties; And see if there is any wicked way in me, And lead me in the way everlasting. (Psalm 139:23–24 NKJV)

Early in the Morning

What are your thoughts when you first wake up? Maybe you linger in bed, wishing you didn't have to get up, or maybe you already have a list of ten tasks for the day. When you develop the habit of setting your morning mind on the Lord, you are beginning your day in the right way.

> Then early in the morning all the people came to Him in the temple to hear Him. (Luke 21:38 NKJV)

March 22

The Appointment

In John 21, the Bible tells us that after Jesus died on the cross, the disciples found themselves in disbelief and disappointment. Things had not turned out the way they'd thought, and quietly, they began to doubt everything they had experienced over the last couple of years. What seemed like disappointment was actually a prelude to the appointment with Jesus! Sometimes, things happen that we don't understand, and we wonder, "Where are you, Lord?"

Jesus is always present. Today, pray that you will recognize your Savior, Jesus Christ.

> Therefore that disciple whom Jesus loved said to Peter, "It is the Lord!" Now when Simon Peter heard that it was the Lord, he put on his outer garment (for he had removed it), and plunged into the sea. (John 21:7 NKJV)

Draw Near

God allows us to receive as much of Him as we desire. We can decide how close our relationships with the Lord will be. God promises that when we take one small step toward Him, He will take a giant step toward us.

You can count on His promise to be true.

> Draw near to God and He will draw near to you. Cleanse your hands, you sinners; and purify your hearts, you double-minded. (James 4:8 NKJV)

March 24

Every Breath You Take

Breathing is something to which we pay little attention, and at times, we take it for granted. On average, we take between seventeen thousand and twenty-three thousand breaths in a day. His breath fills us all.

Pause and focus on your breath in the same way you do your faith. Give thanks to God for breath and for the faith that gives you life.

> The Spirit of God made me, the breath of the Almighty gives life. (Job 33:4 CSB)

Interruptions and Opportunities

Do you view life's interruptions as roadblocks or distractions in your life? Maybe some of those encounters are missed opportunities. Even in the midst of a confusing time, your understanding of Jesus can change the way you receive interruptions and barriers. Jesus was interrupted all the time. He took these as opportunities to give someone a new thought, to change a life. Don't miss your opportunity.

> And Jesus, immediately knowing in Himself that power had gone out of Him, turned around in the crowd and said, "Who touched My clothes?" (Mark 5:30 NKJV)

March 26

It's for a Lifetime

Our friendships are not determined by the number of "likes" we have on Facebook. A true friend knows when we are connected.

Take the time to notice, to take advantage of a text, an email, or even a phone call. This is an opportunity to let the Lord speak through you to others. You have a lifetime to be a friend. Begin now.

> No longer do I call you servants, for a servant does not know what his master is doing; but I have called you friends, for all things that I heard from My Father I have made known to you. (John 15:15 NKJV)

It Matters Who You Love

Sister Mary Virginia believed it mattered to God how we treat people. Her love for the poor was the pure love of Jesus flowing through her. We should always strive to see Jesus in everyone we meet—to love them and treat them with dignity and to give hope. We are all children of God. We should love those who do not have the strength to love themselves. Sister Mary Virginia shared this love with everyone till the day she died, March 27, 2020.

> For I was hungry and you gave me food, I was thirsty and you gave me drink, a stranger and you welcomed me, naked and you clothed me, ill and you cared for me, in prison and you visited me. (Matthew 25:35–36)

March 28

Connect the Dots

At times, life can seem like a series of unconnected dots. In reality, the dots are on your map for a reason. There is a thread of purpose that runs through every moment of your life. Look back through the path your life has taken. Identify the critical points where you turned left or right, answered the text or didn't. See the Lord's thread in each step, each dot. You will find your true path in the Lord.

> You intended to harm me, but God intended it for good
> to accomplish what is now being done, the saving of many
> lives. (Genesis 50:20 NIV)

Laugh Out Loud

Laughter is an emotion God has given us from the laughter part of His own character. We can use laughter to calm our souls.

Don't let the circumstances of life keep you from seeing the humor in your days. The Lord is showing you parts of yourself that you can strengthen—and laugh while doing so. What makes you laugh? When is the last time you laughed so hard that tears were in your eyes?

> Then our mouth was filled with laughter, And our tongue with singing. Then they said among the nations, "The Lord has done great things for them." (Psalm 126:2 NKJV)

March 30

Do What You Know to Do

We know the right thing to do in most situations. Why, then, do we choose not to do it? Making excuses and justifying our inability to act can become a pattern in our lives. The long-term effect on our souls soon wears us down. Making too many excuses will blunt God's emotional, physical, and spiritual plan for our lives.

Live your life free of excuses. Rely on the Lord for the right answer at the right time.

> The sluggard says, "A lion is outside; I might be slain in the street." (Proverbs 22:13 NABRE)

It's in Our DNA

Sometimes our self-esteem can be damaged by an event from our childhoods or the struggles we have faced as adults. Either circumstance can lead us to believe we are not enough and do not deserve the full promises of God. God does not limit His promises. Fulfilling His promises is a true part of His DNA.

> But let justice roll on like a river, righteousness like a never-failing stream! (Amos 5:24 NIV)

I am forgiven because God made me worthy.

—DWC graduate

APRIL

I am ready to die.

Drinking felt like a cold rain shower on a hot day, so very refreshing. I considered myself a social outcast, and drinking was a way to lower my inhibitions. I was the life of every party, as long as I had my dearest companion, alcohol. This friend loved me, never left me, and made me feel superior to the confusing world around me. I was raised in the church by a godly family, so I had no real excuse for drinking, other than it flat-out made me feel good. As long as vodka was my rear guard, I was on top.

I knew something was terribly wrong when I drank for the first time and went straight into the dark hole of a blackout. My beautiful, popular friends in high school were curling their hair and giggling at the prospect of a glorious night with boys and booze while I sneaked in several shots in my "pregame" fashion, just to be comfortable enough to walk out the door. High school came and went like the leaves on a tree in fall. My friends moved on with their lives, leaving me stuck in the bottle.

I was pregnant by the time I was twenty-three, and the new life inside of me gave me a solid reason to do something radically different. It forced me to step into a sense of normalcy that was terrifying. I didn't know what to do without my longtime friend, alcohol. My first marriage to my son's father was a failure; so much hurt and discord on both sides caused us to part like the Red Sea. We were on opposite ends of the middle, never seeing eye to eye and hurting each other in actions and words. After my divorce, I lost myself between the sheets of random men in a vain attempt to feel something—anything! My old friend had returned to join me in my escapades, and the alcoholism intensified to the point where I was hiding in bathrooms and closets, downing gulps of whatever was nearby, just to face the room of people waiting on the other side of the door.

I found my second husband in the multitude of men that paraded past me daily; I fell in love instantly. When we found out we were expecting another child, the prospect was exhilarating but not enough to stop my mischief. I continued to drink while pregnant, and only by the grace of God was my second son born completely healthy. Guilt, however, wrecked me to my core for what I know should have been. I wasn't content with the miracle of his life. My husband begged me to go to treatment once he figured out that I was breastfeeding our child while entirely intoxicated, but I was floating down the river of denial in a boat meant for one.

If I had to choose between alcohol and *anything*, I would select alcohol every time. I found ways to end my marriage because the alcohol whispered sweet nothings in my ear and spun lies into truth. Everything beautiful became ugly; everything that was ugly was now beautiful. Alcohol always won.

Each time I was left alone to my own devices only proved to everyone around me that my life was in shambles. I held down an excellent job for over sixteen years, somehow fully functioning in my dysfunction. The farthest thing from reality was that I thought I had it all together just because I had a home and custody of my two boys. I drove my children in the car while intoxicated and in blackouts. I fought my older son when he would try to take my drinks away with all his little might. I lost myself to the darkness of shame and remorse when I would wake up to my dose of reality.

It wasn't long before I found myself completely alone. The very thing I wanted to succeed in the most, motherhood, was stripped from me, and my sons were removed in the blink of an eye. There were no more nights of me singing sweet lullabies, no more precious coos coming from the crib, no more laughter on the good days, and no more crying on the days I can't even remember. I suffered from a broken heart and empty arms. Depression was a warm blanket I put over myself to forget my pain, and I quit work so I could drink my sorrow into oblivion.

I was homeless and alone when I moved in with a friend. I drank daily from the time I awoke until I could no longer stand. I would fall into a heap on the first surface available, wake up in a fog, rinse, and repeat. The daily agony of wanting to die led me to supplement my alcohol with marijuana and pills. Nothing worked to change the way I felt.

On the Friday before Easter, I had an opportunity to visit with my boys, then aged fourteen and five. My mom came to the obvious conclusion that I was already three sheets to the wind by lunch, so my visit was subsequently canceled. I didn't deserve it anyway. How unfortunate that the very thing I wanted most in life was the catalyst for my drinking, which, in turn, took my babies far away from the arms that desperately wanted to hold them. I was done in, and the torment of my soul took full reign. Hopeless, I saw no way out. I assumed my children would be better off without me. Good Friday found me in the ICU, attached to a ventilator after seventy-five Xanax pills and a bottle of whiskey threatened to snuff out my very existence. Death was forthcoming. I was lying in a tomb of my own making, oblivious to the terrible reports being spoken to my family by doctors who saw that there was no way I was going to live. My prognosis was meager, at best. My family was told to begin making arrangements for my funeral, but the Lord was at work on my wounded heart.

Three days later, on Easter Sunday, to the bewilderment of neurosurgeons and nurses, I woke up. Jesus said, just as He did to Lazarus, "Terra, come forth."

That day, death was arrested, and my life began. God's timing is perfect. On the day I was resurrected to new life, my whole outlook changed. I went straight from social anxiety to a desperation to love others unconditionally—and against my own will, it seemed. The Lord broke through my stubbornness when I could no longer fight, strapped to beeping machines, so that He could perform a miracle beyond scientific explanation. I was released from my chains, a prisoner no more!

My brother found out about the Downtown Women's Center through a series of fortunate events, and he delivered me right into their loving arms. I have since found myself in a new state of normal, quiet, and stillness before the Lord, for He is jealous for me. I believe with all my heart that the Lord did not drag me out of Hades into His marvelous light to leave me now. Restoration will come to my family. Even though my older son says I am not his mommy anymore, I have peace, knowing that God brought His own Son home to Him, so He will bring my son home to me. This time, when my boy graces my door, he will see a woman on fire for the things of heaven and not a drunk, passed out on the floor.

I am set free!

A Promise of Beauty

Everyone looks forward to springtime. There is a promise of beauty in every blossom and the buds in a flower garden. Before we can even see fruit on the tree or baby birds in the nest, we rejoice and have confidence in tomorrow. Be reminded during this beautiful time of year that Jesus is faithful, and hope is found each day.

> Even the wilderness and desert will be glad in those days. The wasteland will rejoice and blossom with spring crocuses. Yes, there will be an abundance of flowers and singing and joy! The deserts will become as green as the mountains of Lebanon, as lovely as Mount Carmel or the plain of Sharon. There the Lord will display his glory, the splendor of our God. (Isaiah 35:1–2 NLT)

April 2

Tell Me Something Good

Do you remember the feeling you had when you received good news? Exhilaration swept over you, and a sense of peace evoked a smile. Good news brings hope and encouragement. It gives you confidence in who Jesus is and motivates you to share it with others. Look for the good news in your life, and go tell someone!

> How beautiful on the mountains are the feet of those who bring good news, who proclaim peace, who bring good tidings, who proclaim salvation, who say to Zion, "Your God reigns!" (Isaiah 52:7 NIV)

To Lead with Love

Serving the Lord was not something Sister Mary Virginia just did as a nun. It was in her DNA since her birth on April 3, 1926. Her love was patient and kind. God blessed her with the gift of mercy toward others, and she didn't pass judgment on their behavior. She calmly shared in their pain and led them with her love. Sister Mary Virginia involved the ladies in serving; she showed them that they always would have purpose in the eyes of the Lord.

> For I know well the plans I have in mind for you—oracle of the LORD—plans for your welfare and not for woe, so as to give you a future of hope. (Jeremiah 29:11 NABRE)

April 4

Where I Belong

The need to belong to something bigger than ourselves is a part of who we are. We find our identities in our social groups. We adapt our beliefs to the cultural traditions of our causes. We belong to Christ, which gives us the opportunity to be a part of His greater cause. His cause becomes our cause as we pursue His character and nature.

> Those who belong to Christ Jesus have crucified the flesh
> with its passions and desires. (Galatians 5:24 NIV)

Knowledge Is Power

We know knowledge is power. The strength of that power is determined by the power's source. We teach what we have learned. Every day, we continue to learn more of the Lord's way in our lives. The power that comes from His lessons is infinite. His power will change us to be our true selves.

> Therefore I will teach them—this time I will teach them my power and might. Then they will know that my name is the Lord. (Jeremiah 16:21 NIV)

April 6

Close Encounter

Every time we encounter the presence of the Lord, we are greeted by His love. Often, we may not notice the wave of love that precedes His voice. It was His love and grace that brought us to say yes to Him in the first place.

Pray to stay connected to His powerful love, as you were in the beginning.

> This is love, that we walk according to His commandments.
> This is the commandment, that as you have heard from
> the beginning, you should walk in it. (2 John 1:6 NKJV)

The Help

Why is it so difficult to ask for help? Maybe it is because we don't want to bother anyone, or pride gets in our way. But what if free help was available to us to solve any problem? Would we be humble enough to ask?

Now is the right time to whisper the prayer, "God help me." He has promised to be an ever-present help in time of need. You can count on the Lord.

> I lift up my eyes to the mountains—where does my help come from? My help comes from the Lord, the Maker of heaven and earth. (Psalm 121:1–2 NIV)

April 8

Just Dance

From the beginning of time, dancing has been a part of many families and cultures. Birthday parties, weddings, and a host of events are celebrated with dancing. Even the youngest of children love to dance. Maybe dancing is one of God's mysteries for healing the weary soul.

When you feel like things are moving in the wrong direction, turn up the music and dance.

> Again I will build you, and you shall be rebuilt, O virgin of
> Israel! You shall again be adorned with your tambourines,
> And shall go forth in the dances of those who rejoice.
> (Jeremiah 31:4 NKJV)

Give It Away

There is a spiritual concept of giving away when we may be in need of so much ourselves. We comfort ourselves when we despair or become blinded to the blessings that come with our giving. When we have a physical or emotional need, and we have Jesus in our lives, we always have something to give, and we are never in lack.

> Give, and it will be given to you: good measure, pressed down, shaken together, and running over will be put into your bosom. For with the same measure that you use, it will be measured back to you. (Luke 6:38 NKJV)

April 10

I Will Remain Confident

Life can feel as though we are weaving our way through a series of barriers. We try to take the right steps, but sometimes we are shaky in our decisions and uncertain of the outcome. A certainty is present when we place our confidence in the Lord. He becomes the confidence we need. He will safely lead us through our challenges to overcome our barriers.

> For the LORD will be at your side and will keep your foot
> from being snared. (Proverbs 3:26 NIV)

Nothing Is Wasted

There is a beautiful story in the Bible about a woman at Bethany who poured her most expensive gift of perfume over the head of Jesus. It was all she had, and her desire was to give it to her Lord. Those who witnessed this act of love were indignant and thought the costly gift was wasted on Jesus.

Sports teams, entertainers, and possessions receive our devout loyalty, and generally, we receive nothing in return. When we pour our praise on Jesus, nothing is ever wasted!

When you pray, don't worry about what others might say. To Him, it is a good work.

> But Jesus said, "Let her alone. Why do you trouble her? She has done a good work for Me. For you have the poor with you always, and whenever you wish you may do them good; but Me you do not have always. She has done what she could. She has come beforehand to anoint My body for burial." (Mark 14:6–8 NKJV)

I Am Secure

In turbulent times, we search for peace and security, never realizing these are parts of us that we already possess. Living our lives from a place of spiritual peace provides us the best way to see our busy world and know where we fit in it. We can stay in His security, knowing that in the midst of a storm, we can trust Christ, and His love will be our dwelling place.

> The work of righteousness will be peace, And the effect of righteousness, quietness and assurance forever. My people will dwell in a peaceful habitation, In secure dwellings, and in quiet resting places. (Isaiah 32:17–18 NKJV)

Release It

Never give up. Don't quit. These encouraging words have been repeated often, motivating us to keep moving forward. But in Christ, the most powerful words we can say are *I surrender.*

Release yourself to the love, hope, and blessings of God. Surrendering to God doesn't mean you give up. It means you release control and depend upon the Lord for the right outcome for the right reasons.

> Cast your burden on the LORD, And He shall sustain you;
> He shall never permit the righteous to be moved. (Psalm
> 55:22 NKJV)

April 14

Tears of Joy

Tears are a response to a decision or challenging news, felt by all of us at some point in life. Tears may come from a physical injury or the loss of someone precious to us. We have all felt tears because we are joyful. In any event, it is OK to cry. The Bible tells us that Jesus wept, but we do not know for how long. Maybe He wept as He was affirming His purpose for which God sent Him.

Let your tears come as you affirm your own purpose for which God has called you.

> Those who sow in tears Shall reap in joy. (Psalm 126:5 NKJV)

Be Persistent

Answers to everyday struggles can be found in the same faith you proclaimed before the struggle. The power of God has not moved as you searched for Him during these times of stress, anxiety, and worry. Be close to the Lord. In this way, you will feel His power and experience His protection. This is how to overcome events and thoughts that challenge your faith. Hang in there. Continue in the Lord.

> For whoever is begotten by God conquers the world. And the victory that conquers the world is our faith. (1 John 5:4 NABRE)

April 16

Our Part Is to Desire

It is our responsibility to determine the type of character that defines us. We can have hearts joined with God's plan for us. We can have spirits that are immovable from His presence. We can have power from the Holy Spirit that restores us to joy. Our part is to desire and make our decision to walk in His way. So, walk on.

> Create in me a clean heart, O God, And renew a steadfast spirit within me. Do not cast me away from Your presence, And do not take Your Holy Spirit from me. Restore to me the joy of Your salvation And uphold me by Your generous Spirit. (Psalm 51:10–12 NKJV)

April 17

Light in the Darkness

There is a uniqueness to light that arouses our curiosity. We can see the light, but the particles that make up the light are invisible. The light that empowers our lives shines forth not only in our lives but also through the lives of others. Darkness cannot remain when the light that is in us brightens a room. Shine on.

> In Him was life, and the life was the light of men. And the light shines in the darkness, and the darkness did not comprehend it. (John 1:4–5 NKJV)

April 18

Be the Example

Have you ever felt God's love, peace, and joy so strongly that you knew your place in God's plan for you and your family? If so, you knew at that moment that the heart of Jesus is the path you are to follow.

When we encounter people whose walk with the Lord is different from ours, we walk the path Jesus has given us, trusting the Lord's role in everyone's path. We invite others to witness the power and the peace of God's path.

> I have given you a model to follow, so that as I have done for you, you should also do. (John 13:15 NAB)

Elevate Your Belief

Striving for stuff can be a perpetual cycle of always wanting. If we are not careful, this striving will influence our spiritual lives. Contentment is a form of God's peace that keeps us balanced. We should strive to know more of the Lord's way and His plan for our lives. We should reach up and grab the higher, satisfying fruit of the Lord.

> Not that I am speaking of being in need, for I have learned in whatever situation I am to be content. (Philippians 4:11 ESV)

April 20

The Game of Life

In the game of life, we sometimes get thrown a curveball. We may feel like a strikeout is next. Unexpected surprises can slow us down. We adapt, we pivot, and we step back up to the plate, knowing there is no defeat with Jesus. No matter what is thrown our way, we will stay close to Him and follow His ways. There is no better way.

> Through You we will push down our enemies; Through Your name we will trample those who rise up against us.
> (Psalm 44:5 NKJV)

Access Granted

Amusement parks and concert events offer total access and special privileges when we pay extra money. The opportunity to go to the front of the line, have VIP seating, or meet the band is granted because we paid the price. Jesus paid the ultimate price on the cross for us so that all can have complete access to God the Father at any time.

Don't just pray to your Savior on holy days. Make every day a holy day.

> Therefore, having been justified by faith, we have peace with God through our Lord Jesus Christ, through whom also we have access by faith into this grace in which we stand, and rejoice in hope of the glory of God. (Romans 5:1–2 NKJV)

April 22

A Way Out

Adversity can come in many different forms. The struggle can be with finances or relationships or in our emotional or physical health. Whatever the trial, we have a way of finding our way through. Where we fix our eyes will be our source of energy, our strength.

Look to God first for the answer and the right path. He will show you the way.

> No trial has come to you but what is human. God is faithful and will not let you be tried beyond your strength; but with the trial he will also provide a way out, so that you may be able to bear it. (1 Corinthians 10:13 NABRE)

What's in My Eye?

When we allow our faith to become off-center, we may become judgmental of family or others. One way we know we are off-center is that we lose our connection to the divine spark that brightens our lives. To regain the divine spark, we ask God for His presence and His help. It is pleasing but not a surprise to be reminded that it is by giving ourselves in service to others that our own pieces come back together, brightened once again by the divine spark.

> How can you say to your brother, 'Brother, let me take the speck out of your eye,' when you yourself fail to see the plank in your own eye? You hypocrite, first take the plank out of your eye, and then you will see clearly to remove the speck from your brother's eye. (Luke 6:42 NIV)

April 24

It Never Lasts Forever

If you have ever walked on the beach in the cool of the evening and heard the sound of the waves, you know that this sound can be soothing to your soul. During a storm, those same waves become so powerful and are capable of massive destruction. Soon the storm will pass, and those waves will become still.

Life can simulate the crashing of waves, but by the power of God, we are assured we will know the calm and peace of gentle waves again. The Lord will be here when the storms pass.

> He calms the storm, So that its waves are still. (Psalm 107:29 NKJV)

Wondrous Works

The ability to be thankful for the goodness of God is, at times, the opposite of what we sometimes feel. It can be difficult to speak the words *thank you, God* because we do not always see God standing with us.

In every moment, good and bad, remember the wonderful way God has led your life. His goodness will always be a way of life you choose and show to others.

> That I may proclaim with the voice of thanksgiving, And tell of all Your wondrous works. (Psalm 26:7 NKJV)

April 26

Acceptance

Life events and decisions come to us all. Sometimes, we are encouraged but not always. We look for acceptance from our friends, our families, and our coworkers. At times, when we are not accepted as we might want to be, we remind ourselves that we are always accepted by Christ. Knowing this gives us the compassion to accept others in the way Jesus accepts us. We pass on what we are given, and to be given the grace of God makes the passing on easy to share.

> Therefore welcome one another, just as Christ also welcomed you, to the glory of God. (Romans 15:7 CSB)

The Power of the Holy Spirit

If we fully understood the power of the Holy Spirit, we would not spend another day worrying. The Holy Spirit fills us with joy, peace, and hope when we need "the feeling" the most. His power sustains us through the toughest of times and gives us the strength to keep moving forward.

Acknowledge the Holy Spirit and feel His power in your life, every day and in every way.

> Now may the God of hope fill you with all joy and peace
> in believing, that you may abound in hope by the power
> of the Holy Spirit. (Romans 15:13 NKJV)

April 28

Desire to Be Healed

Healing can be different for each of us. When it comes to being well—physically, emotionally, or spiritually—making the decision to be well is our responsibility. When we can truly answer that question, we will be on a path to believing that healing physically, emotionally, or spiritually is what we desire and what the Lord desires for us too.

> Heal me, LORD, that I may be healed; save me, that I may
> be saved, for you are my praise. (Jeremiah 17:14 NABRE)

Run Your Race

In baseball, our eyes are on the player at bat. The batter wants to connect with the ball, to hit a line drive or a home run. When we say yes to the Lord, we are at bat in a spiritual sense. Remember there are other people with us on the bases, and there is a crowd in the stands, cheering us on. Most of all, there are no errors on God's team. Just look at the scoreboard.

> Therefore, since we are surrounded by such a great cloud of witnesses, let us throw off everything that hinders and the sin that so easily entangles. And let us run with perseverance the race marked out for us. (Hebrews 12:1 NIV)

April 30

Patience Always

God's message is that we are always remembered, never forgotten. During moments, even long moments, of discouragement, our trust, our faith is in the Lord. We are promised that God knows our journeys, our challenges.

Lean into that trust and be patient. You will not be disappointed. Promise!

> But I trust in your unfailing love; my heart rejoices in your salvation. I will sing the Lord's praise, for he has been good to me. (Psalm 13:5–6 NIV)

Jesus commands us to love God with all we have and to love our neighbors as ourselves. That is what DWC does every day.

—DWC board member

MAY

I am full of misconduct.

I grew up in a conservative Baptist home and was the middle child of seven, born to a police officer family.

An older man lived next door to us in a trailer on the quiet street where I grew up. He decided that it would be a good idea to molest not only me but also my sister and her friend. Molestation at such a young age is somewhat confusing. It awakens deep emotions and strange feelings that should not be felt by anyone so young. The end to that sad, sick drama came when he got caught with the other two girls, doing the things that caused such awful shame. I was at a friend's pool when I overheard my parents' provisional plan to take the other girls to the sheriff to file a report. I mentioned to my parents that I, too, needed to see the sheriff, but they blew off my request as four-year-old antics, and I was unheard for the first time in my life.

My older sisters always blew me off, and my brothers wouldn't accept me as one of their own, no matter how hard I tried, so I felt utterly alone, left out, and truly in the middle of nothing. I was fifteen when, in home economics class, a teenage boy shared with me how I could get high on triple C's (Coricidin HBP Cold and Cough Medicine), so at lunch, I tried it for the first time—the first time but definitely not the last. One thing led to another, and I was getting high on pot, drinking as often as possible, and tripping out on triple C's every chance I got. My parents were clueless about how to handle my new state of mind, but they attempted with all their might to "fix" me every way they knew how; this, however, only fueled my desire for more.

I often moved to escape prying eyes, then eventually joined the army and ran away for good. The prying eyes returned in the form of the federal government. I received an Article 15 for drinking underage in the barracks. But that Article 15 didn't stop them from sending me to Cuba to work as a prison guard, which is when my drinking ensued. Waking up in a strange man's bed in a dark room in Cuba, without a clue how I got there or what I had done, was terrifying but still not enough to keep me sober.

Changing posts to near Seattle was somewhat of a reprieve. I tied the knot with a fellow army soldier from Cuba in his parents' living room in Wisconsin without my parents' consent or their presence. How could they consent when I was already with child? What a travesty, in their minds.

Because I'd made a mistake, I was ignored by people who raised me and were supposed to care for me, but that was something that, unfortunately, I became used to.

I had my daughters in the three years we were stationed in Washington, and I stayed on the sober side of things; that is, until my husband said, "I will watch the girls for you. You should go out and have fun with your friends." I heard the key to my destiny with alcohol and drugs unlock, and I bolted out the door to find peace in the bottom of a bottle and local pharmacy aisles. Marriage was difficult at best, but we were destined to fail when we added a tour to Afghanistan into the fire already brewing, which meant leaving our girls behind. We were in the same company overseas, but we could not be in the same platoon because we were married, so we were ships passing in the night on opposite shifts. After the tour, the reunification process back stateside was quite an ordeal. Our children barely knew us, and we suffered in silence from the effects of the sights no one should ever see.

I began using pain medication to numb myself from the stress of a new life and a new baby that was on the way. I was in blackout nearly every day. When my son was born, my husband became aware of my drug use during pregnancy, but I still felt like a super-stealth concealer of all things obvious, and I thought I could camouflage reality, like I did my own body under battle dress uniforms. I was in combat still but this time in my soul. My husband had no other option but to choose our children over me, and I am grateful that he did. Our divorce and custody war only pushed me farther into darkness. No matter how much I wanted to stop using, it seemed a never-ending battle that I couldn't win. *More* was never enough for me.

Our divorce was interesting, to say the least. Since we had no family nearby, we lived under the same roof. I caught an assault charge for hitting him during a fight, and that was the last straw. He mentioned more than once that if I cooperated, we could get back together, but it was only a façade to get what he wanted out of our nasty proceedings. He moved his girlfriend in quickly after I moved out, then married her a short time later. I was replaced so easily, it seemed. I felt as small as an ant in this great big world when she took over the role of mama to my littles. The army soon decided to send me packing with "patterns of misconduct," and I was discharged to go live the life I felt I deserved. It was just another nail in my house of failure. I saw my kids one summer and put the drugs down in an attempt to prove that I was OK, but cocaine and meth called to me in the night, and I was back on the train to ruination as soon as they departed my sight.

I had been living at my recently deceased grandmother's house, but my parents soon made me abandon the safety of those four walls when I chose my party friends and drugs over stability. I boomeranged from place to place on the streets for eight months, then found myself standing at the mall while my so-called friends stole my car from right under my nose. I crawled back home and hooked up with a controlling lunatic who watched my every move. He chased me down streets to bring me back into his web of deceit anytime I tried to escape his eyes. I had no choice—I could yield to his ways or pay the consequences. I learned quickly that if you give it away, no one can take it, and that is how I dealt with the daily rapes. If I was good enough, I would be worthy enough for him to get me high.

I would go weeks without showering and would end up in the middle of the great outdoors in the canyons, running from people who were not there, begging God for light to see how much dope I was shooting into my arms. The more heightened my paranoia, the more demonic things around me became. Seeing dark shadows and hearing growling became almost normal for me, and it was menacing. When I looked in the mirror, I looked like an eight-year-old Grim Reaper, so the sinister terrors of the night seemed to fit my new-but-not-improved characteristics.

I wanted to die, but I couldn't bear to take myself out. I thought about my children and that they wouldn't even grieve me because I wasn't around them anyway. I contemplated this on more occasions than I should have and mulled it over until I decided that suicide wasn't on the menu. Enough was finally enough. It was then that I willingly submitted my catastrophic life to the Veterans Administration, and they immediately took charge of my case and helped me find the Downtown Women's Center.

There is no doubt that this is where I am supposed to be. After taking time to meditate on my life and the turn of events that led me to this beautiful place of peace, I realized that God saved my life one day in the middle of my divorce. I had a plan to leave work at lunch, go home to our house full of loaded guns, and take my life because it was already over, as far as I was concerned. Right before I got to the road where I would have no cell service, my phone rang, and my dad, said through tears, "I had a dream last night that you took your own life, and I am scared that one of these days we will get that call that you are dead by your own hand." He made me promise that I wouldn't do anything that day, and I kept that promise. Only a loving heavenly Father can orchestrate such perfect timing. I don't think I am where I should be in my walk with the Lord, but God has given me revelation knowledge of His Word that magnifies my soul on a daily basis. God showed me a journal that I wrote while still on the street. I wrote in it, "God is going to start with my eyes. He is going to give me a new way of thinking and teach me what I do not know." Only one page of writing in a notebook of empty sheets, but God was speaking prophecy over my future, and I don't even remember writing it.

I am redeemed!

Take a Stand

It seems like everywhere you look on social media, people have an opinion on just about everything. God's Word tells us we should stay with the truth. Be sure you place your life, your hope, and your word on what is right and good. Be comfortable within your own spiritual skin.

> Stand therefore, having girded your waist with truth, having put on the breastplate of righteousness. (Ephesians 6:14 NKJV)

May 2

With God's Support

Have you ever thought about what true nurture is? There are times when family, work, and even friend issues can overwhelm you. With God's support, you can maintain the practice of nurturing others and your own faith practices too. All this is not easy. The good news is that you do not work your practice alone. Look around. God is present.

> How wonderful and pleasant it is when brothers live together in harmony! For harmony is as precious as the anointing oil that was poured over Aaron's head, that ran down his beard and onto the border of his robe. Harmony is as refreshing as the dew from Mount Hermon that falls on the mountains of Zion. And there the Lord has pronounced his blessing, even life everlasting. (Psalm 133 NLT)

Willingness + Obedience = Blessing

Have you heard about a child who was constantly getting out of his seat, and finally, the teacher told him to sit down and stay? The child replied, "I'm sitting down on the outside, but I'm standing up on the inside."

How many times do we obey God with our spiritual arms crossed? We need a reminder that our heart attitudes are really our messages to God. We are sitting down, dear Lord, arms uncrossed, fully ready for Your presence.

> If you are willing and obedient, you shall eat the good things of the land; (Isaiah 1:19 NIV)

May 4

Sword or Stone

Have you ever tried to do something the way you were told to do it? The account of David and Goliath is a story you may know. David knew what to do. He came with five stones and a slingshot, and the rest is history. The giant fell, and the enemy forces fled. This story tells you to go find the right stones; have courage. Whoever or whatever you are facing, God stands with you. Do not be surprised by what greatness happens next.

> David fastened his sword to his armor and tried to walk, for he had not tested *them*. And David said to Saul, "I cannot walk with these, for I have not tested *them*." So David took them off. Then he took his staff in his hand; and he chose for himself five smooth stones from the brook, and put them in a shepherd's bag, in a pouch which he had, and his sling was in his hand. And he drew near to the Philistine. (1 Samuel 17:39–40 NKJV)

Get Up

Have you stumbled and fallen in public?

Sometimes we have stumbles and falls in our Christian lives too. We can get up, make it right with the Lord, and get on with our days. As believers, we are meant to move forward with the good plans God has for us. God is calling us to get up when we stumble and fall spiritually. He is reaching out His hand.

Take it, rise, and continue on.

> No, dear brothers and sisters, I have not achieved it, but I focus on this one thing: Forgetting the past and looking forward to what lies ahead. (Philippians 3:13 NLT)

May 6

Cut Loose

Have you ever watched a hot-air balloon team prepare for a launch? It is a picture of how God desires to lift us out of our earthly "tie-downs" and the thrill of God being our pilot. When you are feeling weary about financial, social, or physical health, you can call on God to renew your balloon. As you pray, invite the Lord to launch your faith with Him. And upward you go.

> But those who trust in the Lord will find new strength. They will soar high on wings like eagles. They will run and not grow weary. They will walk and not faint. (Isaiah 40:31 NLT)

Joyous Blessings

Sometimes, we have blah days. Maybe your blah day is about an ache or pain or a family member. Perhaps you feel stuck relationally or even spiritually. Think of someone you know who is going through a hard time, and invest prayer time on that person's behalf. God said He will meet all of your needs, so trust Him to lead the way and be the light on the path for your friends and family.

> To all who mourn in Israel, he will give a crown of beauty for ashes, a joyous blessing instead of mourning, festive praise instead of despair. In their righteousness, they will be like great oaks that the Lord has planted for his own glory. (Isaiah 61:3 NLT)

May 8

To Save a Life

Recently, a woman had to have emergency surgery. The surgery went well, and she recovered. Most times, we go forward but not always. Sometimes we need help. Pastors, spiritual support groups, and our own families can be there for us, for us to have long and healthy lives.

> For though I am free from all men, I have made myself a servant to all, that I might win the more; and to the Jews I became as a Jew, that I might win Jews; to those who are under the law, as under the law, that I might win those who are under the law; to those who are without law, as without law (not being without law toward God, but under law toward Christ), that I might win those who are without law; to the weak I became as weak, that I might win the weak. I have become all things to all men, that I might by all means save some. (1 Corinthians 9:19–22 NKJV)

How Rich We Are

We are blessed with the fullness of the Lord.

Share what has been real to you. God will use your story to bless others and you as well. Blessings to all. Keep your life free from the love of money, and be content with what you have.

> "Never will I leave you; never will I forsake you." (Hebrews 13:5 NIV)

May 10

Window to the Soul

When is the last time you looked long and deep into someone's eyes? God shows you the heart of the person's soul through his or her eyes.

By increasing our understanding of someone else, we will become more patient, supportive, and compassionate. When God looks into our eyes, we hope He will see our growth in understanding and compassion as well.

> The lamp of the body is your eye. When your eye is sound, then your whole body is filled with light, but when it is bad, then your body is in darkness. (Luke 11:34 NABRE)

Seasons Change

Many times, after a holiday, stores place seasonal items on sale. Who wants jingle bells at Easter or valentines at Thanksgiving? Sometimes, all this is humorous. Sometimes it's a time to plant or harvest. Sometimes it's a time to know the joy and a time to dance. Let the Lord guide you as you step in and out of the seasons of your life, knowing that He will keep you in perfect peace through all the seasons.

> For everything there is a season, a time for every activity under heaven. (Ecclesiastes 3:1 NLT)

Release It

Have you ever attended a party that had helium balloons? Sometimes, they are released into the sky to float away. Release your worries and concerns to the Lord and see each drift away, not to return. With a balloon, look upward. With the Lord, look inward.

> You have granted me life and favor, And Your care has preserved my spirit. (Job 10:12 NKJV)

Suddenly

We all have family, work, and life challenges in our daily lives. There may be tall mountains of concern or valleys of worry. We may look for an answer on a website or by talking with a close friend. These are helpful and even good. Each talk, each prayer will lower the mountain and fill in the valley.

What works best for you and your family?

> And suddenly, a woman who had a flow of blood for twelve years came from behind and touched the hem of His garment. For she said to herself, "If only I may touch His garment, I shall be made well." But Jesus turned around, and when He saw her, He said, "Be of good cheer, daughter; your faith has made you well." And the woman was made well from that hour. (Matthew 9:20–22 NKJV)

May 14

Coming of Daybreak

After many hours of night driving, we begin to anticipate daybreak. As the light begins to shine through, we gaze upon the beautiful colors of the sun rising to brighten our day. In the same way, we wait for the Lord's light to shine on our paths, even on our darkest days. Daybreak is coming. The light of faith is bursting forth.

> I wait for the Lord; my soul waits and I hope for his word. My soul looks for the Lord more than sentinels for daybreak. More than sentinels for daybreak. (Psalm 130:5–6 NABRE)

Knowing You Are Safe

Have you ever awakened in an unfamiliar place and could not remember, at first, where you were? Sudden events, like job loss or family death, can create a short-term faith gap. Your faith has not left you. God has not moved away. Lean into all you know of your God and let His sustaining power remind you that you are safe and well.

> Watch, stand fast in the faith, be brave, be strong. Let all *that* you *do* be done with love. (1 Corinthians 16:13–14 NKJV)

Being Prepared to Serve

A sports coach will tell you that training, equipment, and teamwork are essential for being prepared for whatever may come. It is the same when you prepare spiritually. Prayer, studying the Word, and practicing compassion are parts of your training program. Share your knowledge and the strength of your faith with family, friends, and work peers. As you prepare, you serve best.

> We are human, but we don't wage war as humans do. We use God's mighty weapons, not worldly weapons, to knock down the strongholds of human reasoning and to destroy false arguments. (2 Corinthians 10:3–4 NLT)

Meeting Goals

Have you ever had a goal of losing five or more pounds by a certain date? Your determination is strong on day one, day two, and even day five. At some point, old behaviors come back, and you are tempted by all the fast foods, pizza, and more. You can ask the Holy Spirit for support to move forward to your goal date. The most fun is to celebrate meeting your physical and spiritual goals. Celebrate. Then, set your goals on new dreams. God is your cheerleader.

> No trial has come to you but what is human. God is faithful and will not let you be tried beyond your strength; but with the trial he will also provide a way out, so that you may be able to bear it. (1 Corinthians 10:13 NABRE)

May 18

Have Faith in Hope

We live in an age where we want instant gratification. We seem to have less patience for the time it takes to receive a home delivery or for a change of behavior in ourselves and others. Discouragement can cause us to give up. If what we are doing is of the Lord, we keep at it with faith.

Being tired is natural; losing hope is not. Keep doing what is right and pleasing to God, and leave the outcomes to Him.

> For in hope we were saved. Now hope that sees for itself is not hope. For who hopes for what one sees? But if we hope for what we do not see, we wait with endurance. (Romans 8:24–25 NABRE)

See the Light

Have you ever used a flashlight? The Holy Spirit is that light in the dark room.

As we stay close to God as our power source, we can see best. We might stumble sometimes, but we will not fall because His light shines the way.

> But all things that are exposed are made manifest by the light, for whatever makes manifest is light. (Ephesians 5:13 NKJV)

Seeing Angels

We do not always know what to do next—that's a good and right time to recognize "angel moments." Angels can be a friend's encouraging word, a meal with a friend, or an unexpected email.

> And when they could not come near Him because of the crowd, they uncovered the roof where He was. So when they had broken through, they let down the bed on which the paralytic was lying. When Jesus saw their faith, He said to the paralytic, "Son, your sins are forgiven you." (Mark 2:4–5 NKJV)

Follow His Pattern

Sometimes we repeat thoughts and actions over and over. When we match our thoughts and actions to the Word of God, we make adjustments; we become better people. What we focus on, we become. Our focus on God's wisdom becomes the wisdom we share with others.

> Therefore, I urge you, brothers and sisters, in view of God's mercy, to offer your bodies as a living sacrifice, holy and pleasing to God—this is your true and proper worship. Do not conform to the pattern of this world but be transformed by the renewing of your mind. Then you will be able to test and approve what God's will is—his good, pleasing and perfect will. (Romans 12:1–2 NIV)

May 22

Keep Your Balance

There is an act in which a performer spins four or five plates on top of narrow poles using a small stick.

All of us do our best to maintain family, work, and personal situations, like the spinning plates. God knows and understands what is on our plates. His peace is our true point of balance.

Pay attention to God, even in the midst of your own spinning calendars, tasks, and family obligations.

> These things I have spoken to you, that in Me you may have peace. In the world you will have tribulation; but be of good cheer, I have overcome the world. (John 16:33 NKJV)

It Matters to Me

People have physical, emotional, and spiritual needs. God wants us to partner with Him to meet these needs. How we treat those around us matters to God. First, we have to see the people all around us. What is a need each may have? Doing for others without expecting anything in return is how we live daily. Needs do not pick and choose favorites. We all experience a time when we have a need.

Trust God's people to be there for you, with you, in every way.

> And the King will say, 'I tell you the truth, when you did it to one of the least of these my brothers and sisters, you were doing it to me!' (Matthew 25:40 NLT)

Show Me Your Glory

What is the biggest request you have made of the Lord? Maybe you prayed about physical or emotional health. When was the last time you made a spiritual ask? The power of the Lord is found in His goodness, grace, and compassion. These are human gifts of the Holy Spirit. Practice each daily.

> So the Lord said to Moses, "I will also do this thing that you have spoken; for you have found grace in My sight, and I know you by name." And he said, "Please, show me Your glory." Then He said, "I will make all My goodness pass before you, and I will proclaim the name of the Lord before you. I will be gracious to whom I will be gracious, and I will have compassion on whom I will have compassion." (Exodus 33:17–19 NKJV)

Hear My Cry

Sometimes life can be downright scary. Maybe not our present moment, but maybe tomorrow looks bleak, filled with unknown outcomes. If we remember in whom we trust and reach out to the One to whom we commit our tomorrows, the world will be calmer and manageable. He is ready to be with us, step by step to all that is safe.

> O God, listen to my cry! Hear my prayer! From the ends of the earth, I cry to you for help when my heart is overwhelmed. Lead me to the towering rock of safety, for you are my safe refuge, a fortress where my enemies cannot reach me. (Psalm 61:1–3 NLT)

Joy Every Day

Why is it, whether small or large, tensions in our daily lives seem like a sore thumb? We may not see the wonder of life anymore. When we take time to notice everyday beauty, we see God's beauty in everything and everyone. As we practice spiritual seeing, our joy will flow, and our strength will remain strong.

> I have told you this so that my joy may be in you and your joy may be complete. (John 15:11 NABRE)

Superpower

Sometimes we may take the Holy Spirit for granted. We expect to have His power but do not dedicate the spirit time to fulfill this expectation. We question why things didn't turn out the way we wanted. When the Spirit of God is our guide, our path becomes smooth, and we know our true direction—and so do the others watching us for their own smooth paths.

> But you shall receive power when the Holy Spirit has come
> upon you; and you shall be witnesses to Me in Jerusalem,
> and in all Judea and Samaria, and to the end of the earth.
> (Acts 1:8 NKJV)

The Fruit of Gentleness

What is your first reaction when communications with a family member, peer, or coworker break down? Sometimes, we forget the right response, thus creating even more problems.

When we decide to walk and talk by the Holy Spirit, kindness and forgiveness become our way, who we really are.

Let the gentleness of the Holy Spirit become your motivation in communications with others.

> Let your gentleness be known to all men. The Lord is at hand. (Philippians 4:5 NKJV)

Love Covers

The concept of unconditional love is difficult to live by. Through the power of the Holy Spirit, we are provided the ability to love others through their faults and failures, just as Jesus loves us through ours. Let's cover each other like an umbrella, with the love that God has given us.

> Above all, let your love for one another be intense, because love covers a multitude of sins. (1 Peter 4:8 NABRE)

The Place of Rest

Think about how it feels after a long day to stretch out and relax. God provides us an opportunity to rest in Him. He will guide us and give us wisdom, and the Holy Spirit will never leave us. With our focus on God, we will find our true rest.

> Take my yoke upon you and learn from me, for I am gentle and humble in heart, and you will find rest for your souls. (Matthew 11:29 NIV)

The Gift of Grace

Going before a judge can be intimidating. We are accountable for our actions or inactions. The cost may be lighter or longer than we first thought. A strong part of faith is not judgment but forgiveness, the grace to accept our imperfections.

Live strong. Show your faith.

> Let us therefore come boldly to the throne of grace, that we may obtain mercy and find grace to help in time of need. (Hebrews 4:16 NKJV)

Knowledge is power and is meant to be shared. God doesn't want us to be stingy with the knowledge He has shared.

—DWC employee

JUNE

I am a career criminal.

I was a good girl, a fine example of what a young lady should be. I excelled in school, graduated from college, and went on to work for Congress in Washington, DC. It was the 1980s, and everyone loved to stand in the newfound freedom that had originated in the decades before. The world around us was at peace under President Reagan, and the District was alive with promise and hope—and parties on every corner. Long hours in the law firm led me to try cocaine, which was incredibly prevalent during that era. Everyone was doing it; it seemed to be accepted by all walks of life, and it didn't take long for me to wind my way down the deadly spiral of drug addiction.

My boyfriend, with whom I was living at the time, introduced me to every drug on the scene. Soon, I knew that if I wanted to live, I needed to run away. I took off for Sacramento to be with my sister. It wasn't long before my boyfriend followed me to the Golden State, and our party picked up where it had left off. We shared the same bed and living space for nearly five years. We were wrecking balls everywhere we placed our feet. Still able to hold down a good job, I considered myself a functioning addict. But every day, once the high heels and stockings were off my feet, the pipe, loaded with crack, hit my lips. Eventually, I put my boyfriend on a Greyhound bus back to Virginia because I was unwilling to share my drugs with him. I was in no shape to handle a relationship with anyone, including my family, with whom I had minimal contact and had not seen in years. It was time to move somewhere else. I had worn out my welcome in Cali.

I moved to New Mexico and moved in with a good childhood friend. I got a good job right away and stayed away from drugs for a brief period. It was there that I realized I could never run from this darkness, so, out of sheer hopelessness, I lost myself to it and ended up using so many drugs that I was very soon homeless, without work, and living on the streets. Every shiny thing passing by looks like a promise when one is without hope. So, one day, I hopped in the back seat of a car with two strange men, and we drove, and drove, and drove into one sunset after another. One of our stops happened to be Amarillo, Texas, where our car died. I had never heard of the town except through men crooning "Amarillo by Morning" through the car's speakers. It didn't take long for me to see that this town offered a new and exciting opportunity because it was easy to be homeless in Amarillo. The possibilities seemed endless, and the help presented by missions, such as Faith City Mission and the Salvation Army, gave me peace of mind, warm food in my stomach, and a comfortable place to sleep on sweltering summer nights.

By 1995, I had a new boyfriend on my arm, and our codependent nature kept us attached at the seams. We were sleeping in our car in Elwood Park. A nun was there with a group that was having a barbecue, feeding the homeless and downtrodden during Easter. The nun walked over to us and asked, "Are you hungry?" We quickly said yes as our bellies grumbled.

She brought us plates loaded down with food and a stuffed bunny rabbit. "You are my two blessed Easter surprises," she said as she handed us our treasure. The nun's name was Sister Mary Virginia. We decided to help this saint of a woman and painted rooms and did odds and ends for her at Abba House. We kept in touch with Sister Mary Virginia. Eventually, we started doing drugs again. Sister Mary gave us a hotel room to stay in for a while. She did her best to lead me back to the church and encouraged me to get back in touch with my family. At this point, I began my life as a criminal—there wasn't too much that I was not willing to try if it got me more drugs. Eventually, of course, I ended up on probation. As much as I loved Sister Mary and respected her tremendous faith and belief that I was a good person—she never gave up on me—I continued my downslide. I had once heard, "You come to Texas on vacation, and you leave Texas on probation." How true that was for me.

I was arrested for felony fraud in Amarillo, as I was collecting food stamps from five different states at the same time. I didn't do well on probation. I violated it more than once and ended up in the Substance Abuse Felony Punishment (SAFP) program in prison. Once I was released, I moved back to my parents' home in northern Virginia and landed suitable employment. I did well for a season, then found myself on the front stoop of my childhood home, being told that I could no longer stay because my relapse was ripping out the hearts of those who loved me the most.

It was then that the bustling streets of Washington, DC, became my new comfort and home away from home. I stayed in crack houses and projects and did everything under the sun to keep myself high and checked out of life. Every Sunday, without fail, my mom would meet me in the District. I would clean myself up enough to meet her at a beautiful church, and afterward, she would buy me a meal, and we would walk and talk. Her heart broke each time she walked away and left me to all that consumed me. One day a week was all she could bear to make sure I was alive. I lived on the streets of DC for over a year.

The state of Texas soon came calling due to another violation of my probation. I was extradited to Texas and spent twenty-nine days in the back of a dogcatcher van, shackled to the walls. I went through the SAFP program once again. The boyfriend I'd lived with in the car at Elwood Park was also in the SAFP program. Upon our discharge, we moved to Austin so that I could go through the transitional treatment center there. Frank and I married in 2000 in Virginia, surrounded by family and friends, and then returned to Austin, Texas, where we began our life as a married couple.

I again scored an excellent job, and we did well for over two years. I violated my probation again, which was a regular pattern after a relapse. I was dragged back to Amarillo against my will. The jail got in touch with Ann Sanders at the Downtown Women's Center, and she offered me an apartment in Abba House, and I began working a recovery program in earnest. I went directly from my rack in jail to a comfortable bed at the Abba House. I worked temporary jobs while Frank held down the fort in Austin. I met a ton of wonderful people. I was very tight with all of my sisters in the program. But true to form and my current recidivism rate, I found myself hitting the pipe once again. I completely fell apart, ended up at the Pavilion Psychiatric Hospital, and lost myself to the world's darkness. I fell to my knees and prayed for God to help me out of my mess.

Diann Gilmore visited me at the Pavilion and asked me point-blank, "What do you want?"

I said, "I really think I need to go back to Virginia to see my parents."

She reluctantly gave me over to my own devices, and I ran away from myself for the last time.

For the first time, I had long-term sobriety and had gotten back into my family's good graces, but then I slipped up and found myself in one of the worst jails in the country in Washington, DC. Going into that jail, I immediately felt the oppression. While I was there, my mother died unexpectedly in November 2003. I wasn't allowed to go to her funeral. My brother and sisters didn't even know where I was! I had never felt as low in my life. I finally realized my bottom. I made a vow that day in one of the darkest places on earth and in my life, and I have not picked up a drug since. That was nineteen years ago.

When I was released from the DC jail, my father was suffering from Alzheimer's and was still trying to figure out for himself where my mother had gone. My brother and sisters didn't have much faith in me. And it was quite the journey to learn how to forgive myself and receive forgiveness from others. I threw myself into anonymous meetings, got a sponsor, got it together, obtained a good job working with National Guard military families for two and a half years, worked at forgiving myself, and gained my brother's and sisters' trust. My siblings and I are now very close, and I have enjoyed being inside now instead of outside looking in. I know that I may have another relapse in me, but I don't know if I have another recovery in me. I remain aware to stay alive.

I have lost friends to relapse and addiction in the past few years. I grieve for them. I know now that I am still here because God has a plan for me. I have a purpose that no one else can do because I am the only person on this earth who is me. I treasure the friendships I have made and am so grateful for these friendships.

Frank and I moved to Georgia and decided to be caretakers for my father. Once in my life, my dad wanted nothing to do with me, and here I was, his caretaker in the last years of his debilitating disease. I walked with the Lord closely during that very special time. For two years, it was just us, laughing and loving one another past the old pain. In 2009, he lost his battle with Alzheimer's disease. My brother and sisters and I did our best to bring joy in Dad's life as a family. He so loved his family. I sometimes get sad and anxious about my strong, beautiful mom and hope she knows how sorry I am that I missed time with her due to my addiction. I believe she looks down and is proud of the woman I strive to be today. I am lucky to be surrounded by my beautiful, strong sisters and amazing brother.

The beach has always been my happy place, and now that I am retired and live in the Florida Panhandle, I spend as much time as possible there, enjoying family. I am so grateful I have been able to have amazing relationships with my beautiful niece and three nephews. I see God at work in my family's joy when we all get together on beautiful St. George Island, Florida, on the Gulf of Mexico.

The beach in Georgia is my happy place these days, where I can seek solitude and find God in everything. I started over with my employment and had to rely on God to put me where He wanted me to be, regardless of my criminal record. He had a plan for me, and I took whatever job I was given while I waited. I spent fifteen years working for Social Security as a disability examiner and am truly grateful for the opportunity to assist others.

I spend my time walking the beach, searching for seashells, taking special care of the broken ones, knowing that these are the special seashells that have survived the rough seas and have come to rest on the peaceful beach.

For me, getting honest was the life-changing moment that catapulted me into the blessings and favor of the Lord.

One of the biggest blessings is that I am now a dependable, reliable individual.

I am a new creation!

Have Mercy on Me

God's mercy may smooth out all that troubles us, even what makes us uncomfortable. His mercy releases compassion and love into our lives. Mercy is given to us because of God's love. We do not earn it. Mercy is a gift, a free gift just for us.

> Have mercy upon me, O God, According to Your lovingkindness; According to the multitude of Your tender mercies, Blot out my transgressions. (Psalm 51:1 NKJV)

June 2

Have a Heart

Often in our prayers, we are not clear on what we want or need. Life's challenges can block our faith and sometimes confuse our beliefs. When we allow the Holy Spirit to teach us and guide us, we live a life that is clear and have a heart that is open to others.

> But without faith it is impossible to please Him, for he who comes to God must believe that He is, and that He is a rewarder of those who diligently seek Him. (Hebrews 11:6 NKJV)

In His Own Image

We can become overly concerned with images of ourselves or others. Jesus showed us how we should live, spiritually and physically.

If your place in your family, work, and community has God as your source, feel secure in who you are. Live in a spiritually and physically healthy way.

> Then God said, "Let Us make man in Our image, according to Our likeness; let them have dominion over the fish of the sea, over the birds of the air, and over the cattle, over all the earth and over every creeping thing that creeps on the earth." So God created man in His own image; in the image of God He created him; male and female He created them. (Genesis 1:26–27 NKJV)

June 4

Pay Attention

Have you ever had thoughts that come out of nowhere? If the thoughts are from God, keep them. If not, touch the delete button. Give God the time to develop your thinking, your thoughts. He is bringing you along in His own way. When you are ready, God is ready too.

> Then your light shall break forth like the morning, Your healing shall spring forth speedily, And your righteousness shall go before you; The glory of the Lord shall be your rear guard. (Isaiah 58:8 NKJV)

Paths

Faith is not stagnant. Our faith is changed, made stronger, through life's challenges. In reading our Bibles, we gain an understanding of how best to live our lives each day. Understanding our lives encourages us with our own challenges. Our faith is increased as we walk our own spiritual paths and show others these same spiritual paths.

> They conquered him by the blood of the Lamb and by the word of their testimony; love for life did not deter them from death. (Revelation 12:11 NABRE)

June 6

Whose Way Is Best?

What do we do when we are unsure about our faith? Our beliefs about God are at the core of who we are. As our faith is affirmed, we see people and events in a new way, a better way, His way. The gifts of the Spirit become forever parts of who we are. And with all that, we are now secure in what we believe about God. This way is the best way.

> For you did not receive the spirit of bondage again to fear, but you received the Spirit of adoption by whom we cry out, "Abba, Father." The Spirit Himself bears witness with our spirit that we are children of God, and if children, then heirs—heirs of God and joint heirs with Christ, if indeed we suffer with Him, that we may also be glorified together. (Romans 8:15–17 NKJV)

Time for Harvesting

Farmers know to gather and bring in their crops. They are prepared to plant seeds and cultivate the soil. We are living in a season where growing a healthy spiritual life can be shared with others. This is our time to gather goodness, not for ourselves but to nurture and strengthen the faith life of others. We are at our best when we live, grow, and raise our families among others.

> These were his instructions to them: "The harvest is great, but the workers are few. So pray to the Lord who is in charge of the harvest; ask him to send more workers into his fields." (Luke 10:2 NLT)

June 8

Like a Good Neighbor

There is a story about a man who knew all the people in his neighborhood. Not only did he know the ones next door, but he knew others down the block too.

Jesus encountered crowds of people, learned people's names, and listened to each story. His love and interest in others showed in how He lived. He expects each of us, as believers, to do the same.

> Jesus said to him, 'You shall love the LORD your God with all your heart, with all your soul, and with all your mind.' This is *the* first and great commandment. And *the* second *is* like it: 'You shall love your neighbor as yourself.' On these two commandments hang all the Law and the Prophets. (Matthew 22:37–40 NKJV)

Notice and Pay Attention

The staff in the Intensive Care Unit monitor their patients twenty-four/seven. God watches over us twenty-four/seven also. We are under His care in the same way we show our care for an elderly neighbor or the young mother balancing her work life and her three kids. As believers, we notice and pay attention, as God pays attention to our families and us.

For many of us, when we first decided to follow Jesus, it seemed like we were in a spiritual ICU. Other believers walked with us, prayed with us, and coached us. As we follow the orders of the Great Physician, we are released in the care of the Holy Spirit. We practice wellness of the body as well as the spirit.

> When Jesus saw him lying there, and knew that he already
> had been in that condition a long time, He said to him,
> "Do you want to be made well?" (John 5:6 NKJV)

God Celebrates Your Joy

In the world of athletes and internet heroes, sometimes our lives may seem small or "less than." God does not see us this way. Every right decision or caring action to others is about joy. There are no small or less-than believers.

Greet every day, knowing your joy is celebrated by God.

Therefore, whether you eat or drink, or whatever you do, do all to the glory of God. (1 Corinthians 10:31 NKJV)

Are Your Shoes Dirty?

While sitting in a doctor's office, a woman noticed a young man wearing the whitest tennis shoes. The shoes were worn but clean. She felt it necessary to comment on them. "How do you keep your shoes so clean?" she asked.

"I don't step in the dirt," he said.

When we serve the people of the Lord, sometimes we do get both our shoes and our spirits dirty. This is where we find the people to be served.

Clean or dirty, if you are helping others in the name of the Lord, all is well. Dirt is OK.

> You are already clean because of the word which I have spoken to you. (John 15:3 NKJV)

Branch Out

In an agriculture ad, a company sold a product that protects the crop's roots. Likewise, our spiritual condition is dependent on healthy roots. It is only by staying connected to Jesus that we are fully healthy. We reach out and touch others as the Lord has touched us and made us whole, roots and all.

> I am the vine, you are the branches. He who abides in Me, and I in him, bears much fruit; for without Me you can do nothing. (John 15:5 NKJV)

Act on Your Faith

Born into homelessness, Carolyn found herself in a shelter at age twenty-five. With little hope, she stumbled into a Bible study at the shelter. Even though she had little money, Carolyn decided to act and made a small donation to the shelter. The shelter staff helped Carolyn find work on a bus line.

Acting on your faith is always the right choice. What do you need to act on today?

> "Bring all the tithes into the storehouse, That there may be food in My house, And try Me now in this," Says the Lord of hosts, "If I will not open for you the windows of heaven And pour out for you *such* blessing That *there will* not *be room* enough *to receive it*." (Malachi 3:10 NKJV)

June 14

Pour Out Love

A young girl was surprised by the balloons and presents she experienced for her first birthday party. Her mother, a shelter resident, wiped away tears. The outpouring of love was overwhelming.

We have our own tears as God continues and continues again to pour out His love and caring for us. His caring is like our balloons and presents. We, like this mother, are grateful.

> And when they had come into the house, they saw the young Child with Mary His mother, and fell down and worshiped Him. And when they had opened their treasures, they presented gifts to Him: gold, frankincense, and myrrh. (Matthew 2:11 NKJV)

Stop, Drop, and Pray

Most of us have met a friend or family member in a public place. That person may share about his or her immediate challenges. Sometimes, we are in a hurry and fail to listen fully.

Although Jesus was interrupted often, He took time to listen. When people ask for prayers, we should stop, listen, and be present with the Lord. This is how we serve the Lord and show His goodness to others.

> Therefore, confess your sins to one another and pray for one another, that you may be healed. The fervent prayer of a righteous person is very powerful. (James 5:16 NABRE)

June 16

The Dawn of a New Day

Every day, we are blessed with an opportunity to begin again. God's grace and mercy is present with us in the night and greets us as we wake. Just as a painter starts with a blank canvas, God is the artist of our life canvases, and the images are beautiful. We all deserve a place on the wall of faith.

> Light is sweet; how pleasant to see a new day dawning.
> (Ecclesiastes 11:7 NLT)

Endurance

There was a younger person who was unhappy with his company's culture. He made the decision to resign.

We place our faith in the Lord. We walk in His path. He stays with us. We stay with Him. Healthy faith makes for the right and good culture. Tell others. All are welcomed.

> We can rejoice, too, when we run into problems and trials, for we know that they help us develop endurance. And endurance develops strength of character, and character strengthens our confident hope of salvation. And this hope will not lead to disappointment. For we know how dearly God loves us, because he has given us the Holy Spirit to fill our hearts with his love. (Romans 5:3–5 NLT)

Receive It

It is exciting to watch a wide receiver catch a seventy-yard pass. Our relationship with the Lord is much the same as the quarterback and receiver. God passes His Word to us, and we have to be open to receive and act on it. When we read and study God's Word, the Holy Spirit will encourage our faith to grow and reach out to others, even those seventy yards away.

> My son, if you receive my words, And treasure my commands within you, So that you incline your ear to wisdom, *And* apply your heart to understanding; Yes, if you cry out for discernment, *And* lift up your voice for understanding, If you seek her as silver, And search for her as *for* hidden treasures; Then you will understand the fear of the LORD, And find the knowledge of God. (Proverbs 2:1–5 NKJV)

Stay Prepared

We prepare for many things. We lay out our plans and the steps it will take for each project. Spiritually, the outcomes we desire happen when we prepare our hearts to hear God's plan. When we submit our plans to Him and then wait for His answer, the Holy Spirit becomes alive in our lives and can be seen by others.

> The preparations of the heart belong to man, But the answer of the tongue is from the Lord. (Proverbs 16:1 NKJV)

Connect to God

When we are finally able to open an internet site, we see the colors and read the information. We are connected in real ways, in real time. In the same way, when our connection to God is secured, our faith is real.

Keep searching, and keep preparing. It is the greatest of times when you are connected.

> For though I am absent in the flesh, yet I am with you in spirit, rejoicing to see your *good* order and the steadfastness of your faith in Christ. (Colossians 2:5 NKJV)

Material Possessions

God desires for us to have material things to enjoy and to make our lives fuller. These "things" are not in our lives to be a barrier to faith. As maturing believers, we know how to balance our lives in what we purchase and within the faith circle of our daily lives of work and family—our wider world.

Enjoy it all, keeping the art of balancing going as it should.

> Jesus said to him, "If you wish to be perfect, go, sell what you have and give to [the] poor, and you will have treasure in heaven. Then come, follow me." When the young man heard this statement, he went away sad, for he had many possessions. (Matthew 19:21–22 NABRE)

Hearing with Your Heart

We can become suspicious when individuals say they hear God speaking to them. When we are open to hearing and to learning, Jesus always speaks. One way we hear God's message is by being still and quiet and opening our hearts.

You may also hear God's voice to you in a market or while exercising. All this is about being open, not a specific place or time. Practice being open to listening, and don't be surprised by what you hear.

> Behold, I stand at the door and knock. If anyone hears
> My voice and opens the door, I will come into him and
> dine with him, and he with Me. (Revelations 3:20 NKJV)

Repentance Leads to Salvation

When things don't turn out the way we wanted, sometimes doubt can overtake our thoughts. Every relationship has times when all is well and times when we could do better. Our relationship with God is no different. The ups and downs of life do not define our faith or our relationships with God. If we temporarily move away from God, He is still with us when we return.

> For godly sorrow produces repentance leading to salvation, not to be regretted; but the sorrow of the world produces death. (2 Corinthians 7:10 NKJV)

June 24

We Are Not Alone

A teacher once said that she had anxiety when her students took their final exams. The stress she felt was for her students.

God has promised He will never leave us. The Holy Spirit is with us, with the assurance that the Lord is with us in stressful times as well as times of joy. He assures us that all will be well.

> The Lord Almighty is with us; the God of Jacob is our fortress. (Psalm 46:7 NIV)

You Can't Take It with You

Look around at your home. Ask the Holy Spirit to help you align your material values with all you know of God's values. When values match values, you can relax. You are making the right decisions.

> Do not store up for yourselves treasures on earth, where moths and vermin destroy, and where thieves break in and steal. But store up for yourselves treasures in heaven, where moths and vermin do not destroy, and where thieves do not break in and steal. For where your treasure is, there your heart will be also. (Matthew 6:19–21 NKJV)

June 26

What's on the Inside

Our relationships with family and friends are based upon our experiences. Mostly, it is about character. If we judge people, we limit our own goodness. Every individual, culture, and family is special to the Lord.

The next time you see someone who may be different from you, look at what's on the inside, accept them as unique to God, and welcome them into your life and your faith.

> Judge not, that you be not judged. For with what judgment you judge, you will be judged; and with the measure you use, it will be measured back to you. (Matthew 7:1–2 NKJV)

First Love

There are times in our walk of faith when we get caught up in doing the work of the Lord. We are faithful to attend church. Yet we lose sight of why we are doing what we do. Our intense faith may weaken over time. The fix is simple. Say hello again, in true faith, and return to His love and guidance.

> Remember therefore from where you have fallen; repent and do the first works, or else I will come to you quickly and remove your lampstand from its place—unless you repent. (Revelation 2:5 NKJV)

Be Open

Responsibilities include family, work, and friends. Not only do we have physical responsibilities, but we also have spiritual ones. We have an obligation to seek guidance from the Lord. Through prayer, the Holy Spirit will bring individuals and truth into our lives.

Don't be fearful of being open with those you trust. God has placed saints around you who support you.

> Arise, for this matter is your responsibility. We also are with you. Be of good courage, and do it. (Ezra 10:4 NKJV)

A Calm Spirit

Wisdom and knowledge together will produce understanding. The daily decisions we make give us a certainty that the Holy Spirit is alive in our lives. When we apply spiritual wisdom, we increase the intimate knowledge of the Lord and His way.

> He who has knowledge spares his words, And a man of understanding is of a calm spirit. (Proverbs 17:27 NKJV)

We Are One

Our beliefs, our faith, and in whom we trust are on display in the words we speak and in our actions. We pray and meditate on the scriptures. When we come together as the body of Christ, we are strengthened, and our families and friends are too. The word *together* is the important faith word.

> I do not pray for these alone, but also for those who will believe in Me through their word; that they all may be one, as You, Father, are in Me, and I in You; that they also may be one in Us, that the world may believe that You sent Me. (John 17:20–21 NKJV)

Once you receive unconditional love, you begin to expect it. —DWC employee

JULY

I am a prostitute.

I should have been on guard from a very young age. I grew up in a single-parent home with an alcoholic mother. My mom used every excuse to drink when she was home. She drank beer and did laundry and made everything look OK. My dad was a successful car salesman and partied like a rock star. We moved a lot for my mom's jobs. I went to live with my dad and stepmother when I was twelve because of the fights my sister and I would have. I had no voice. I was to be seen and not heard. I was expected to perform on every level in my young life. I had to play the part they expected of me, down to the haircuts and clothes I wore.

I knew God from a very young age. He was all I had. I would sing songs to Him in the pasture. In the second grade, I accepted the Lord into my heart in the Church of Christ.

I did what I was told for my entire life. I was molested by one of my dad's friends, a very influential man who hung out with my socialite dad and stepmother. A year later, I wrote a suicide note at the age of sixteen because I had so much resentment. My first blackout drunk was that week. I started looking to party any time my parents were away. Of course, they didn't notice because there was so much alcohol in our home. It empowered me and made me feel like a different person; I finally had an outlet. In my junior year of high school, I put my foot down and requested to move back in with my mother, and they obliged. I was working while getting ready for graduation. After graduation, I thought it would be a good idea to start topless dancing at a club in Arlington, Texas. My lifestyle took a drastic turn.

I put myself in one dangerous situation after another. I had no discernment so I fell for everything. I met my first fiancé at the club. He was in the motion picture industry and was shooting a feature film in Fort Worth, Texas. He moved me to Los Angeles a year later. We were using and drinking together, and for the next nine years, I would have only short periods of sobriety. I held jobs as an administrative assistant for large multimillion-dollar corporations. I met a very well-known actor in a club and was written a $20,000 check and given a Harley motorcycle.

I split up from my fiancé. I ended up as an extra in well-known movies and on the cover of DVDs. I was up and rising in Hollywood, and nothing would keep me down. I did on-and-off jobs throughout my reign in Los

Angeles. I was on fire! I was a Hollywood sunset starlet. My fiancé and I kept trying to make it work. He would beg me to stop drinking. He said he would never say *never* with me, but I could not stay sober long enough to have a lasting relationship. I regret that deeply.

I ran for the next ten years. I found myself back in Texas with only the clothes on my back in the early spring of,1998. In August of that year, I had a near-fatal motorcycle accident. For the next eight to nine months, I suffered from encephalitis (swelling of the brain), and I have scars all over my body from the road rash. I was afforded the opportunity to stay high on pain pills. I kept running from who I was and the wreckage I created in my wake. I started using meth so that I could stay up longer to drink. The booze fueled my pain, and the meth numbed it out. I did not know how to deal with my emotions, and I had no life skills or coping skills to help me survive.

Pride was my best friend. People would give me money just because I was beautiful and fun. I never had consequences for my actions or behavior, other than emotional ones. I moved back to LA and started bartending. My lifestyle was affording me my addiction. I was able to manage and maintain but not without the drama that followed. I had to put on a mask every day just to exist. Sobriety came when I got pregnant with my daughter. She was born in 2007. Her father was extremely abusive, so she and I left on a jet plane back for Texas when she was still an infant. No one wanted us as their responsibility, so we were shuttled around quite often.

I believe that my daughter saved my life. She gave me a reason to live because I had lost the will to live for myself. We ended up staying with friends in a small Texas town. I started drinking again, moved in with a boyfriend, taught him how to use, and violence ensued. I went to my mom's house in San Antonio, but she was still in the bottle. It was nearly impossible for me to stay clean. When my daughter was almost four, we went through a mother-child program. It was faith-based but not recovery-based. As soon as we graduated from that program, I started drinking again. My bottom was not in sight.

I got engaged once again, but it was over before it began. Using a man to survive was not going to be my motivation, especially if that man was mean to my child. I moved, bounced between jobs, lived from pillar to post, and dragged my daughter all over Texas. My child was removed from my home because I couldn't pass a drug test. I was running a full-time prostitution ring out of my house and was making thousands of dollars a night to support my addiction and keep a roof over my head. People were flying in from other states and paying me to be their call girl. I became a professional escort in Kerrville, Texas.

I couldn't complete CPS services in time, so to keep my daughter out of foster care and close the case, I called her dad to come get her and take her back to California. He ended up jobless and homeless in under six months. His mother picked up my daughter and brought her back to Amarillo. The law finally caught up to me in 2015, and I was arrested. The night before, I had asked God to help me change my life. I had started a cycle I couldn't get out of. He hemmed me in, all right, and put me behind bars. I had allowed things into my life and had no boundaries, so I was used and abused by everyone. I was held hostage in my own mind and by people who profited off me, so they surely didn't want me to stop what I was doing. I was grateful to go to jail.

My worth was in the arms of a man in the middle of a business transaction. I thought it would be a good idea to buy a gun and commit suicide. The only thing that stopped me was the thought of someone telling my daughter that I had left her for good. Instead, I pulled a knife on my assistant, who was living with me and helping me get ready for my nights with strangers from foreign places. I'd had enough of her. God used that as a way to answer my prayer.

The doors did not swing wide for me in jail. An angel didn't show up and break my physical chains to walk me out. I got so much *more* than that. I finally had time to rest, contemplate, pray, and seek God with all my heart and soul. My relationship with my heavenly Father was restored in a maximum-security hold. He left me bread crumbs to know there was a pathway to trusting Him again.

I got out of jail and was put on probation. I picked up a drink right away. I didn't know what my day looked like without drugs and alcohol. They signed me up for the prison rehabilitation program. I had no choice but to surrender my will and my life. I was processed in a week before Thanksgiving in 2015. I ended up having surgery to remove my breast implants due to silicone poisoning; they had ruptured and were leaking into my chest wall.

I had written to countless places, trying to get into a program before my release. One of those letters was to the Downtown Women's Center. The letter I received back was more than encouraging. They took me, sight unseen. When I was discharged early, I walked right into the doors of Haven House. When Ramona opened the door at 5:30 a.m., and I fell asleep on the couch in their living room, I knew I was home. What God had for me was so much better than I could have imagined. My daughter has been restored to me. We have a home of our own.

I truly believe that if you cannot get sober at the Downtown Women's Center, you haven't hit your bottom. For the first time in my life, I know what my day looks like sober.

I am whole!

More than Enough

Imagine you are hosting an open house. Your guests are residents of the nearby homeless shelter. The invitations have been word of mouth. The success of this gathering is a faith event, completely in the hands of the Lord. Trust the Lord. Celebrate all who come.

Like the disciples, we often think that what we have in our hands is not enough. The disciples must have wondered how a crowd of five thousand men could be fed with five loaves of bread and two fish. Sometimes, it looks like who we are is not enough, but if we give all we are to Jesus, there will be thanksgiving. He is there for us, and we will find we have more than enough.

> Then He commanded the multitudes to sit down on the grass. And He took the five loaves and the two fish, and looking up to heaven, He blessed and broke and gave the loaves to the disciples; and the disciples gave to the multitudes. So they all ate and were filled, and they took up twelve baskets full of the fragments that remained. (Matthew 14:19–20 NKJV)

Stay Steadfast

Sometimes we are burdened by personal problems or grief from the loss of someone close to us. We may wonder if Jesus knows the burdens of our hearts.

During these times, do not move away from the assurance that God is enough. Be clear in your beliefs. His heart is tuned to you always.

> My heart is steadfast, O God, my heart is steadfast; I will sing and give praise. (Psalm 57:7 NKJV)

God Trusts Us

The scripture tells us to trust God with everything. He instructs us to place our cares with Him. The Lord has chosen us to be His hands and voice on this earth.

Ask the Holy Spirit for the strength to do His will, and allow your purpose to be fulfilled. The Lord trusts us to show His love, joy, and power to change the world. All this begins with you.

> I thank Christ Jesus our Lord, who has given me strength to do his work. He considered me trustworthy and appointed me to serve him. (1 Timothy 1:12 NLT)

July 4

True Freedom

Seeking independence does not always bring freedom. It is through dependence on the Lord that the true height and depth of freedom will be experienced. Freedom in the Lord gives us permission to know a love so powerful that when we share this love with others, they desire to have what we have.

Freedom is not always about doing what you first want to do. Let God's love be the true freedom for which you and your family live.

> For you were called for freedom, brothers. But do not use this freedom as an opportunity for the flesh; rather, serve one another through love. (Galatians 5:13 NABRE)

There Is a Solution

There is a solution to our challenges, and it is found in the Word of God. Our faith is empowered when we pray God's words back to Him.

Allow the Holy Spirit to bring focus to your prayer life. Open your eyes and heart to the answers already before you.

> Rejoice always, pray without ceasing, in everything give thanks; for this is the will of God in Christ Jesus for you. (1 Thessalonians 5:16–18 NKJV)

It's a Habit

Habits are a way of thinking that can take residence in our minds and hearts. Good habits are best. We condition ourselves to believe and act from our habits.

Consider the habits that work for you and those that do not. Good habits are the ones to keep.

> Don't copy the behavior and customs of this world, but let God transform you into a new person by changing the way you think. Then you will learn to know God's will for you, which is good and pleasing and perfect. (Romans 12:2 NLT)

The Will of God

Have you thought of what it means to live in the will of God?

We may believe that only our good acts are within the will of God. When we act with compassion, we are in God's will. When we accept others, we are in His will. Acting on faith is how we know more and more of God's will.

> Now may the God of peace who brought up our Lord Jesus from the dead, that great Shepherd of the sheep, through the blood of the everlasting covenant, make you complete in every good work to do His will, working in you what is well pleasing in His sight, through Jesus Christ, to whom *be* glory forever and ever. Amen. (Hebrews 13:20–21 NKJV)

Help Comes from the Lord

Mountains are magnificent. Their peaks rise to heaven, and our rivers are fed with life-giving water. As we think upon nature, we know our spiritual and physical needs are met through Him. Remember that God made the heavens and the earth. He is able to give us our true lives, just as the mountains are able to give the land water.

> I look up to the mountains—does my help come from there? My help comes from the Lord, who made heaven and earth! (Psalm 121:1–2 NLT)

He Will Do It Again

Holidays can bring forth memories of the best of holidays and some that were not. God, as always, is true in times of happiness and in times of heartache.

Ask the Holy Spirit to remind you of what God has given to you, and be assured He will do it again, even now.

> "We will use these stones to build a memorial. In the future your children will ask you, 'What do these stones mean?' Then you can tell them, 'They remind us that the Jordan River stopped flowing when the Ark of the Lord's Covenant went across.' These stones will stand as a memorial among the people of Israel forever." (Joshua 4:6–7 NLT)

By His Spirit

We often hear the expression "might makes right" in today's world. As a result, bullying, arrogance, greed, and all sorts of prideful attitudes are common. In Jesus's life, there was never room for destructive rhetoric, boasting, or cruelty. As we acknowledge His ways and His thoughts, there will be no limits on what we can accomplish in Him.

> So he said to me, "This is the word of the Lord to Zerubbabel: 'Not by might nor by power, but by my Spirit,' says the Lord Almighty." (Zechariah 4:6 NIV)

Power in Union

There are times when we need a trusted friend to whom we can go for support or to share the happiness in our lives. Jesus told us that He will be with us when we have these times with each other, so make room for one more. We are not alone in our sharing and in receiving support.

Let's talk.

> So you also are complete through your union with Christ, who is the head over every ruler and authority. (Colossians 2:10 NLT)

July 12

Only He Knows

When we look at old family photos, our heritage—our aunts and uncles—also are with us, in many ways, in our future. It is the same with Jesus. He was with us when we were young, and He is with us now. He is with us whether seen in the old photos or not. He was there then, and He is here now.

> Remember the things I have done in the past. For I alone am God! I am God, and there is none like me. Only I can tell you the future before it even happens. Everything I plan will come to pass, for I do whatever I wish. (Isaiah 46:9–10 NLT)

We Are Messengers

As believers, we have the mind of Christ. He gives us wisdom with our daily challenges. Our response to the words and behavior of others may be a reminder to that person; our spiritual calm also can be others' calm as well. Really, in faith, we are messengers. The grace and calm spirit of Christ is our important message.

> Finally, all of you, be like-minded, be sympathetic, love one another, be compassionate and humble. Do not repay evil with evil or insult with insult. On the contrary, repay evil with blessing, because to this you were called so that you may inherit a blessing. (1 Peter 3:8–9 NIV)

The Sound of Power

Power and control are not a good part of any of us. We see the desire by some to control others, whether children and family, employees, or a friend. The sound of power begins with the words we speak and then our actions. The Holy Spirit will lead us to be kind with our words and the same with our actions.

> Death and life are in the power of the tongue, And those who love it will eat its fruit. (Proverbs 18:21 NKJV)

Faith in God

Positive thinking and faith in God are not necessarily the same thing. One pushes us to believe in our abilities; the other pushes us to believe in God's ability. We should never deny our emotional and physical abilities. Our faith and our beliefs are even stronger. Each has a role, a place in our daily lives.

> Jesus said to them in reply, "Have faith in God." (Mark 11:22 NABRE)

Always Present

Sometimes, as we are still or even when we are moving fast, we do so with faith and goodness from the Lord. His Love and His total understanding are with us. Our faith is not only a quiet-time faith. We live in noise, even chaos. God is still ahead of us, waiting for us, always present.

Those who sow in tears Shall reap in joy. (Psalm 126:5 NKJV)

Stay Steady

One of the most popular attractions at an amusement park is the roller coaster. It fills us with excitement. We trust that the giant bolts anchored into the concrete foundation will provide the necessary strength and steadiness to keep us safe. Our faith is both exciting and steady. No matter what, God is always there, giving us strength and keeping us steady.

Amazing, right?

> Suddenly, a fierce storm struck the lake, with waves breaking into the boat. But Jesus was sleeping. The disciples went and woke him up, shouting, "Lord, save us! We're going to drown!"
>
> Jesus responded, "Why are you afraid? You have so little faith!" Then he got up and rebuked the wind and waves, and suddenly there was a great calm.
>
> The disciples were amazed. "Who is this man?" they asked. "Even the winds and waves obey him!" (Matthew 8:24–27 NLT)

July 18

The Gift

Think about a special gift you purchased for someone. Remember the excitement of giving it and experiencing his or her enjoyment of your gift. God's gift to you is His Son, Jesus. Receive this gift into your life in order to fulfill the hopes and dreams that have been placed before you. All you have to do is say, "I accept."

> "For God so loved the world that he gave his only Son, that whoever believes in him should not perish but have eternal life." (John 3:16 ESV)

Strengthen My Hands

When God gives us a dream, an idea, to do something important, it doesn't mean that achieving the dream will be without opposition. In fact, that may be a sign we are doing what God has called us to do.

Your calling is your claim to your future, to your success. So act on your calling. There is greatness ahead.

> For they all were trying to make us afraid, saying, "Their hands will be weakened in the work, and it will not be done." Now therefore, O God, strengthen my hands. (Nehemiah 6:9 NKJV)

Strength and Courage

God wants us to be strong and courageous in the midst of our personal or work challenges. Whatever we can't see around, God can. He brings rest to our unrest, order to our disorder, success from our failures.

Be strong and courageous in your hope and trust in God, and watch Him—and you—achieve greatness.

> So be strong and courageous, all you who put your hope in the Lord! (Psalm 31:24 NLT)

A Matter of Trust

God desires for us to trust Him with our hearts and our lives. He does so because He wants our love, trust, and service to others to be freely offered to Him. We can live each day, trusting God to be a steady God through all of our challenges, feeling His own faith in us.

> And Abraham called the name of the place, The-Lord-Will-Provide; as it is said to this day, "In the Mount of the Lord it shall be provided." (Genesis 22:14 NKJV)

He Gives Life

Nature gives a beautiful image of God's world. A seed is planted; someone does that. Water is provided for that seed; someone does that. Another protects the seed against being choked out by weeds; someone does that. People are put in our lives to help us grow. They are resources from Him to us. The seed, water, and even the weeds are part of His world, now our world to protect and to grow.

> It's not important who does the planting, or who does the watering. What's important is that God makes the seed grow. (1 Corinthians 3:7 NLT)

Listen and Wait

We live in a hurry-up, impatient world: traffic lights or a drive-through with eight cars. Many times, our faith is not patient. We want to know everything now and want that matched to our priorities. Waiting on the Lord is a great life lesson for us to learn.

Listen. God is waiting for you.

> Wait for the LORD; be strong, and let your heart be courageous. Wait for the LORD. (Psalm 27:14 CSB)

Reset

Have you ever awoken with negative or anxious thoughts? Perhaps at other times you might feel arrogant or self-righteous.

We can reset our hearts and renew our minds by turning our thoughts to Christ. It is through Him that our worth and value are made known. All of us need reset buttons.

> He saved us, not because of the righteous things we had done, but because of his mercy. He washed away our sins, giving us a new birth and new life through the Holy Spirit. (Titus 3:5 NLT)

Present in Real Time

Eight-year-old Jerome turned to his mother to ask, "Why doesn't God have a Facebook page? I've been searching but no God." The mother was quiet, unsure how best to answer. She could tell she had better have a real answer to her son's real question. "Honey, God's Facebook page is in our hearts, harder to find at first, but He never goes away into the blue sky."

Whether your God is online or offline, He is present with you in real time, always.

> And it is impossible to please God without faith. Anyone who wants to come to him must believe that God exists and that he rewards those who sincerely seek him. (Hebrews 11:6 NLT)

July 26

Finding Our Way

We thought we had challenging days before, but none like these times. We use our "now-time" to listen and gain His wisdom in making sense of the news. We see many others also struggling with this same now-time. What a unique time to share our faith to give hope and strength to others. We are in this together, each finding our way.

> Hear attentively the thunder of His voice, And the rumbling *that* comes from His mouth. (Job 37:2 NKJV)

Gather Together

As Christ-followers, God never ever meant for us to live and work alone.

To keep connected, reach out and call or text a friend today. If you're on a walk, wave to a neighbor, or shout out a greeting. Staying connected can take many forms. Find the one best for you. God is present, both today and tomorrow.

> Be kindly affectionate to one another with brotherly love, in honor giving preference to one another; not lagging in diligence, fervent in spirit, serving the Lord; rejoicing in hope, patient in tribulation, continuing steadfastly in prayer; distributing to the needs of the saints, given to hospitality. (Romans 12:10–13 NKJV)

July 28

In You

Pressure is something that affects all of us. It can come from wrong thoughts inside of us, other people's expectations of us, or from circumstances in our lives. It is important for us to stop, not to react or despair but to look to God, who is in us. His Word is truth, and through it, we can recognize and overcome the lies and deceit that so easily invade our lives.

His strength in you is strong. Trust the Lord.

> You, dear children, are from God and have overcome them, because the one who is in you is greater than the one who is in the world. (1 John 4:4 NIV)

Two Powerful Words

In the midst of challenges, trusting God can be hard to do. We want a place that is familiar, out of uncertainty, out of our pain and weariness. God always moves us forward. He has our future in mind and knows where He wants to take us and what it will take to get us there. The essence of our faith is trusting God. No matter the situation, we believe the two powerful words—trust God.

> Trust in the Lord with all your heart; do not depend on your own understanding. Seek his will in all you do, and he will show you which path to take. (Proverbs 3:5–6 NLT)

July 30

Help Me, Lord

Often, we find ourselves in situations that have the potential to overwhelm us. We are not sure what to pray for or how to pray. At times, the Lord lays individuals on our hearts, and we want to pray for them. Not knowing the entirety of the situation, we may lack confidence, which causes us not to trust the prompting of the Holy Spirit. God knows this, and the Holy Spirit will help us during these times.

It is in your weakness that God is made strong, so be encouraged when you don't know what to pray. Keep your heart turned to the Lord because He knows every situation.

> And the Holy Spirit helps us in our weakness. For example, we don't know what God wants us to pray for. But the Holy Spirit prays for us with groanings that cannot be expressed in words. (Romans 8:26 NLT)

First Things First

What is your morning routine? Do you turn on the coffee? Check social media? Head for the gym? Before you do any of that, begin your day with God. Ask for His guidance in your day. By doing so, the Holy Spirit will guide your thoughts and actions so they match with His. This simple little act will become a meaningful beginning of each morning

> The one thing I ask of the Lord-the thing I seek most-is to live in the house of the Lord all the days of my life, delighting in the Lord's perfections and meditating in his temple. (Psalm 27:4 NLT)

My whole life has changed. I'm doing things today I never thought I would or could ever do.

—DWC graduate

AUGUST

I am in pain.

My story was a jumbled mess in my head until recovery, but that's when the Lord brought clarity to so many things that were utterly abnormal in my life, things that I was unaware of. Now that I have a deeper understanding, I can speak of this drama as it unfolded and start at the beginning of my pain.

I was raised in Tulia, Texas. I had a pretty good childhood until I was eight years old. At that time, I was the victim of sexual abuse. I never told my parents because I didn't want them to be hurt like I was, grieving the offense. I grew up in the early '70s, and no one taught me about what was appropriate behavior and what wasn't. It seemed normal to me because no one had told me otherwise. I just stuffed the memories of those dark days into the closet of my mind and moved on with life. My dad was a raging alcoholic from the time I was eight until I was twenty-one. My mother did not get out because she wanted to stay for my sake. She was not able to leave, so she stuck it out, as some wives do. His mental, physical, and verbal abuse took a significant toll on my psyche.

I always felt that I wasn't good enough, smart enough, or pretty enough for my dad's affections to fall on me like rain. I stood alone most days and endured the bullying at school like a champ. I became involved with men as I grew into my teenage years and gravitated toward ones who beat me down or beat me up, for that was all that I knew. By the time I was nineteen years old, I was so full of anxiety that I started pulling my eyelashes right out of my eyelids. It was merely a symptom of the inner pain I felt inside.

I always believed that God was with me. I prayed daily to my Lord and Savior when I was growing up. Still, I had no idea that harming my body was out of the realm of a so-called normal existence.

I married a cheating, abusive man and had a few children with him. Our marriage, which was built on unsteady shores, came crashing down when the winds of adversity blew in with hurricane force. I dealt with life in the best way I knew how—by hiding my true self from everyone close to me. I was a successful nurse and a good mom. My dad had always told me never to rely on a man to take care of me, so education and self-reliance were easy paths to take. I took care of my children without the help of others, which only magnified the anxiety disorder I was suffering from. I was eventually diagnosed with trichotillomania after pulling all the hair out of my scalp, one strand at a time. Finally, I had to wear wigs to cover my baldness.

I started drinking to mask the pain emanating from every pore in my body. I would drive my children to school when I was drunk. One day, I drove my son to school a few blocks away and left my daughter at home in bed to sleep. When I got home, I passed out in the driveway and awoke to my baby girl banging on the car door and crying, wondering why I wasn't waking up. That was a reality check for me.

I was heavyset and had gained a lot of weight. I found that getting diet pills from the doctor was a great way to ease the anxiety, give me confidence, and help with my bad self-image. I would take Lasix before seeing this doctor to show that I had dropped a few pounds so that he would prescribe me more of this new wonder drug. Again, I didn't see this as a problem, just a means to an end.

I ended up weighing well over three hundred pounds. I decided to have gastric bypass surgery and dropped eighty pounds. I felt better, and I looked better. My friend's brother had just been in treatment for drugs in Lubbock. He was adorable, he liked me, and we hit it off. I thought it would work since he was on the road to recovery, but that was the farthest thing from the truth. I believed that the love of a good woman would keep my man on the straight and narrow. I soon realized that you can never bring a person up to where you are; they always bring you down. Using methamphetamines became my new "normal."

I couldn't keep gainful employment, and my priorities were completely skewed. I begged, borrowed, and stole to get high, no matter the cost. I got sucked right into spiritual warfare, justifying every move I made farther into the despair of this horrible life I was now living. I thought I could win over my man and get him away from his mistress and meth, but I found out that drugs don't let you love anything but drugs. As hard as I tried to get him to love me, nothing worked. I couldn't stay clean. I was arrested two or three times for stealing from Walmart and placed on probation.

My house became a swinging door for anyone and everyone who wanted to come in. My daughter was not even a teenager, and I was subjecting her to evil every time the hinges creaked. IV drugs were prevalent in my very living room. The police always looked for the rejects and hardened criminals who darkened my door. The cops eventually raided my home, after telling my neighbors to stay somewhere else for the night in case of a shootout. I was charged with possession of a controlled substance. My daughter and her dad drove by just as the cop handcuffed me and placed me into the patrol car.

I was bonded out and awaited a court date for well over a year, which gave me more than enough time to continue ruining my life. I was put on probation but could not stay clean for the life of me. I played the games with my probation officers to get by but had no intention whatsoever of staying on the straight and narrow. I figured I wasn't hurting anyone but myself, but in reality, I was harming everyone who dared come near me. After four failed drug tests, my probation officer had finally had enough. The noose around my neck was tightening, and I could hardly breathe. She sat me down, looked me dead in the eyes, and talked to me like a mother and a human, not like an offender. She spoke to me about the Downtown Women's Center. I begged her to leave me alone, but she refused. She started asking hard questions: "What is going to happen to your daughter if you don't get your life together? What is going to happen to your nursing license? What about the people who love you? What about them?"

She reached me on a different level. She implored me—mother to mother, one caring soul helping another—to give it a chance. She told me what I needed to do to get into DWC and gave me step-by-step instructions. On August 3, 2014, I walked into Haven House and began my journey. I was not happy; I was very prideful and scared silly. I thought I was different from the other women in the program until it registered with me that pain is universal. The hurt is the same, and the fear is the same; the darkness is the same, regardless.

Child Protective Services (CPS) had taken control of my family situation. They cornered my daughter in school and told her that I had a drug problem and that they were going to take her. Yet she still believed in me and had faith that I could change. I had qualified myself to fall under every entity imaginable. The State Board of Nursing, CPS, drug court, ARAD (Amarillo Recovery from Alcohol and Drugs), and the Downtown Women's Center monitored me. Every day for the first four to six months at Haven House, I had to meet service requirements for one of the above. It was the hardest I have ever worked for anything in life. I finally realized the truth of the matter through countless counseling appointments set up for me by the different organizations that kept a close watch on my recovery process. My childhood sexual abuse was the root of it all. I lost my identity in that process and never found it again until Jesus showed me how. The little girl inside of me never had a chance. She never felt good about herself in the world; she feared abandonment and rejection and fought like mad to be released from the prison I had put her in long ago.

I couldn't believe God would allow me to start a new life without a dime in my pocket. In the Downtown Women's Center restroom, a plaque on the wall read, "Acceptance can do more for you than your willpower can ever accomplish." That phrase hit me squarely between the eyes, and pride melted away. I prayed for God to give me peace and patience. I never wanted to cause my daughter another ounce of pain. To do that, I had to submit to spiritual authority, become teachable, and learn how to do battle in the space between my ears. The devil comes to steal, kill, and destroy, and I refused to lie down and take that.

I am now five years clean of drugs and have started my new life in recovery. I found a gentleman to marry with over twenty-four years clean. My story is not over; it is ongoing until the day I die. I am closer to God now than I have ever been. My daughter has graduated from high school and is going to school to study to be a veterinarian. When asked about our experience, she bravely said, "If you had never gone through this, Mom, I wouldn't be the person I am today."

I am set apart!

August 1

Valleys and Mountains

We all understand the valleys of life. There is comfort in knowing the achievements of the mountain are matched by the surrounding comfort of the Lord in the midst of our daily challenges, our valleys. We are not left alone to wander. God is on the path, being present with us.

Through both valley and mountain, God is with you. Walk on.

> Even when I walk through the darkest valley, I will not be afraid, for you are close beside me. Your rod and your staff protect and comfort me. (Psalm 23:4 NLT)

True Partner

Work, church, or community meetings have an agenda. Your spiritual life also can have an agenda. Your agenda may be coffee with a friend; family or personal challenges; prayer and conversation about God's goodness; or simply being alone. It is in paying attention to all the parts of you that God is found—your true partner. Say hello.

> "For where two or three gather in my name, there am I with them." (Matthew 18:20 NIV)

August 3

He Can Handle It

God delights when we place our plans and our burdens before Him in prayer. The act of turning over, of letting go, shows our faith in God's plan.

Practice the giving up, the letting go, in order to receive His peace. The yielding to Him will give you the certainty of His love and the grace to live your faith life each day. What do you need to let go of today?

> Now to Him who is able to keep you from stumbling, And to present *you* faultless Before the presence of His glory with exceeding joy, (Jude 1:24 NKJV)

Jesus, Our Friend

We see and talk with many people during the day. They may see us in a hallway or in passing at church. We are at our best when two or more are our trusted friends. Together, we understand our past and claim our peace in the present and our common hope for the future. Acting and listening about God, with faith, becomes the way we live, worship, and serve others.

> No longer do I call you servants, for a servant does not know what his master is doing; but I have called you friends, for all things that I heard from My Father I have made known to you. (John 15:15 NKJV)

August 5

Teach Me to Love

If we desire to live in faith, we fulfill God's trust in us to love those around us, to love the ones whose names we do not know, who are forgotten or left behind, and yes, those who have harmed us in some way. As we practice love, the Holy Spirit will give us patience and wisdom. He will fill our days with kindness, compassion, and prayers for others.

> Dear friends, since God loved us that much, we surely ought to love each other. (1 John 4:11 NLT)

Let It Rain

When trouble comes all at once, the bills are due, your job is not all you want, and your body feels the stress, take a breath. Join with others. Share your challenges. This is the meaning of *fellowship of believers*. Together, you are an umbrella for whatever rain may come. In faith, stronger days are ahead.

> For I will pour water on him who is thirsty, And floods on the dry ground; I will pour My Spirit on your descendants, And My blessing on your offspring; They will spring up among the grass Like willows by the watercourses. (Isaiah 44:3–4 NKJV)

August 7

Stay Connected

The anticipation of reconnecting with someone you haven't seen in far too long creates excitement and joy. The same is true when you drift away from the Lord's peace and then return, seeking the peace and understanding you know is best for you and your family. So, reconnect. Feel the spiritual excitement and joy of true fellowship.

> Now may the Lord of peace himself give you his peace at
> all times and in every situation. The Lord be with you all.
> (2 Thessalonians 3:16 NLT)

Firm Foundation

"The Three Little Pigs" is a children's story that depicts the consequences that come with building a home on a faulty foundation. The wolf was able to destroy all the homes except for the one built with bricks. Our spiritual lives and where we build our trust is much like this children's story. When the storms come, it matters which foundation we have chosen to build upon. Trusting in the power of God is the only foundation that will withstand every storm.

> When the earth quakes and its people live in turmoil, I am the one who keeps its foundations firm. (Psalm 75:3 NLT)

Lessons Learned

The Bible is full of stories of people used by God to change the world. Whether it is the leadership of Moses, the reign of King David, or the bravery of Esther, their stories provide life lessons for all of us. These individuals, however, can't change our situations, hear our prayers, or save our lives. Only Jesus has the power to do all those things. We should look to Him as our example of how to walk this life by faith. Maybe the lesson we should learn from Moses, David, Esther, and others is to keep our eyes on the Lord.

> Therefore I will look to the Lord; I will wait for the God of my salvation; My God will hear me. (Micah 7:7 NKJV)

Gentle Whisper

Jesus never pressures us or overpowers us. Many times, we ignore His whispered guidance to follow Him. Sometimes, we might need to turn off the TV, put aside office work, and go to our prayer spots to seek His healing, peace, and joy. His love completes our hearts and strengthens our spirits.

> "Go out and stand before me on the mountain," the Lord told him. And as Elijah stood there, the Lord passed by, and a mighty windstorm hit the mountain. It was such a terrible blast that the rocks were torn loose, but the Lord was not in the wind. After the wind there was an earthquake, but the Lord was not in the earthquake. And after the earthquake there was a fire, but the Lord was not in the fire. And after the fire there was the sound of a gentle whisper. (1 Kings 19:11–12 NLT)

August 11

Worship

Today, ask yourself if there are ways you can improve your worship and your following of the Lord in your life. The benefits to you will build upon each other, all adding to your joy and your relationships with family, work, and church. All the parts of you and of your faith now will come together in new and better ways.

> Oh come, let us worship and bow down; Let us kneel before the Lord our Maker. (Psalm 95:6 NKJV)

Be Led

The Spirit of God will never lead us to sin because it is not in His character and nature. His Spirit can only lead us to His truth, and that truth is always found in the Bible. If we want to know when we are being led by the Spirit of God, we must know what the Spirit of God would do, and that is always found in Jesus. It's not enough to simply know Jesus; we must have a deep desire to be like Jesus. The Holy Spirit will fulfill that desire in us, and our character and nature will change. His character will become our way of life.

> If we live in the Spirit, let us also follow the Spirit.
> (Galatians 5:25 NABRE)

August 13

Choose This Day

Have you ever met people who serve others from the depths of their hearts?

Serving others is a leadership quality that all great leaders possess. They aren't born with it; they choose it. We have all heard someone say, "I serve the Lord." In fact, most believers have spoken these words but have given little thought to what serving the Lord really means. Serving the Lord is more than attending church, going to another Bible study, feeding the poor, or giving money. All of these are great things to do, but maybe the best way we can serve the Lord is to lead family and others to Jesus.

> And if it seems evil to you to serve the Lord, choose for yourselves this day whom you will serve, whether the gods which your fathers served that were on the other side of the River, or the gods of the Amorites, in whose land you dwell. But as for me and my house, we will serve the Lord. (Joshua 24:15 NKJV)

Hope Road

Taking the wrong road while traveling across the United States, before GPS, was pretty common. Asking the gas station attendant or reading a map was your only hope of finding your destination. When circumstances cause you to lose your way and hope is hard to find, you can ask the Holy Spirit to guide you to your destination. You will find the road back to hope because He is your true hope and guide.

> I pray that God, the source of hope, will fill you completely with joy and peace because you trust in him. Then you will overflow with confident hope through the power of the Holy Spirit. (Romans 15:13 NLT)

August 15

Good News

Waiting on results can be difficult. While hoping for good news, our minds can wander to the negative. Good news is not something for which we have to wait. Waking up in the morning, God gives us His breath for another day. Facing the daily challenges in life, God gives us His strength. Don't shy away from sharing the wonderful blessings of God and the good news of Jesus Christ.

> How beautiful on the mountains are the feet of the messenger who brings good news, the good news of peace and salvation, the news that the God of Israel reigns! (Isaiah 52:7 NLT)

Shield of Protection

Often when we hear the word *protection*, we think of physical protection. God is a shield in our lives that protects us from taking the wrong job, getting in a wrong relationship, saying the wrong thing, or believing lies. His protection, in a thousand ways, is available to us through His Word.

Know that you walk within His shield of protection.

> Every word of God proves true. He is a shield to all who
> come to him for protection. (Proverbs 30:5 NLT)

August 17

Simplicity

There are parts of us that we can improve and strengthen to be pleasing to God. His wishes for us are simple and within our abilities. Staying focused on God's true way is what works, day in and day out.

Today, there's no need to complicate your faith life. Today, follow all your knowledge of God's truth—a simple and rewarding day ahead.

> No, O people, the Lord has told you what is good, and this is what he requires of you: to do what is right, to love mercy, and to walk humbly with your God. (Micah 6:8 NLT)

Merciful Kindness

God's mercy shows up in the kindness of others, and He meets us on the road we are traveling.

In this season, take a few minutes and think about your own journey. If there was a time when God poured His merciful kindness on you, find a way to show kindness to others. Don't allow yourself to think that you have nothing to give; when you have Jesus, you always have something to give.

> For His merciful kindness is great toward us, And the truth of the Lord endures forever. Praise the Lord! (Psalm 117:2 NKJV)

August 19

His Rest Is Available

Rest is not something we enter into easily. We work late, take care of our homes and families, and take care of laundry and an evening meal. At some point, we seek rest from all that our days have been. Even in our being tired, we should end our evenings with thankfulness. This is the best path to rest. By being thankful, we restore who we are for the coming day and who we will meet along the way.

> There remains therefore a rest for the people of God. For he who has entered His rest has himself also ceased from his works as God did from His. (Hebrews 4:9–10 NKJV)

Redeem the Time

The way we spend our time is important. In addition to work and family, we give to ourselves by nourishing our spiritual lives, whether with a pen and journal, a paintbrush, music, or a walk in the park. We may also care for a neighbor or friend with physical needs. It is by the giving of ourselves that we receive even more. And for this, we are grateful.

> See then that you walk circumspectly, not as fools but as wise, redeeming the time, because the days are evil. (Ephesians 5:15–16 NKJV)

August 21

The Gift of the Sabbath

The Sabbath for Christ-followers is a day of rest, generally observed on Sunday. Today, in our faster, twenty-four/seven world, rest is hard to find. Adding a slow-down part of our week is important for our spiritual, emotional, and physical health.

If you work on Sunday, your Sabbath can be Tuesday or Friday. Jesus is Lord of your Sabbath, whatever the day. His promises are a part of this faster, challenging world. Find your place. You are not alone.

> Then Jesus said to them, "The Sabbath was made to meet the needs of people, and not people to meet the requirements of the Sabbath. So the Son of Man is Lord, even over the Sabbath!" (Mark 2:27–28 NLT)

He Listens

There are times when we don't know what or how to pray. We feel that the Lord is silent, and our prayers seem unanswered.

When you find yourself just going through the motions, and you don't know what to pray, keep praying. Pray with faith, knowing the Lord listens and pays attention, as you also listen and pay attention to Him.

> I prayed to the Lord, and he answered me. He freed me from all my fears. Those who look to him for help will be radiant with joy; no shadow of shame will darken their faces. In my desperation I prayed, and the Lord listened; he saved me from all my troubles. For the angel of the Lord is a guard; he surrounds and defends all who fear him. (Psalm 34:4–7 NLT)

Peace Over Fear

Searching for wisdom is a lifetime endeavor. Proverbs 3:21 tells us to "maintain sound wisdom and discretion" as we journey through life.

If the past year has been riddled with fear, make the decision today to seek the peace that wisdom provides, which only can be found in the Word of God. Step into the new season with trust and confidence, knowing that the Lord will keep you in perfect peace. His Word becomes your lifeline.

> Maintain sound wisdom and discretion. My son, don't lose sight of them. They will be life for you and adornment for your neck. Then you will go safely on your way; your foot will not stumble. When you lie down, you will not be afraid; you will lie down, and your sleep will be pleasant. Don't fear sudden danger or the ruin of the wicked when it comes, for the Lord will be your confidence and will keep your foot from a snare. (Proverbs 3:21–26 CSB)

Peace Is a Place

Peace is a place where we can travel any day, any time. There is no need to take sick leave or vacation or ask permission. We don't have to take our families or pack a bag. The accommodations are always prepared for us. Pray, be mindful of Jesus, and relax in perfect peace.

> "With firm purpose you maintain peace; in peace, because of our trust in you." Trust in the Lord forever! (Isaiah 26:3–4 NABRE)

It's in the Giving

Through realizing the mighty strength of Jesus, the securities, delights, and cares of this world become foggy and dissipate. We are not called to live an easy life, but one that can be full of joy—the kind that doesn't depend on circumstances, feelings, or finances. It is built on knowing Jesus.

Reach out to someone and, in doing so, receive the promise that it is only in the giving that you receive. This is His way to a full and joyful life. Receive—and give—all that He has for you, each and every day.

> Give, and it will be given to you: good measure, pressed down, shaken together, and running over will be put into your bosom. For with the same measure that you use, it will be measured back to you. (Luke 6:38 NKJV)

Ever Ready

We know it's important to keep the electronic devices and tools in our lives charged. It is even more important to keep ourselves charged and ready. Eating healthy food, getting enough sleep, and exercising make us ready. We also need to be ready mentally and emotionally, but the best way is our relationship with Jesus Christ.

Spend time with His Word, in prayer and in listening for His voice. The Holy Spirit will lead and guide you into all truth.

> Finally, draw your strength from the Lord and from his mighty power. (Ephesians 6:10 NABRE)

Who Is He to You?

At times, reading the Bible can be an item to check off the list so we can move into our day. Giving deep, meditative thought to the words will help us gain more insight into the meaning of the passages.

Make it your goal to open your heart and mind so that the messages can be fully received. Let His words live in your spirit, and take time to determine who He really is to you.

> He has delivered us from the power of darkness and conveyed us into the kingdom of the Son of His love, in whom we have redemption through His blood, the forgiveness of sins. He is the image of the invisible God, the firstborn over all creation. For by Him, all things were created that are in heaven and that are on earth, visible and invisible, whether thrones or dominions or principalities or powers. All things were created through Him and for Him. And He is before all things, and in Him all things consist. And He is the head of the body, the church, who is the beginning, the firstborn from the dead, that in all things He may have the preeminence. (Colossians 1:13–18 NKJV)

Crisis of Faith

On occasion, we all have questioned ourselves and our faith. Mother Teresa privately struggled with her faith. Jesus prayed that He be spared from suffering crucifixion. We are human, and Jesus experienced His humanity and the full weight of our sins when He cried and asked God why He had been forsaken when He died on the cross.

When you find yourself in a crisis, surround yourself with others whose love for Jesus will inspire you to share. Having questions does not keep God from loving us.

> "For a mere moment I have forsaken you, But with great mercies I will gather you." (Isaiah 54:7 NKJV)

He Rewrites Our Stories

Feeling inadequate and unworthy of the love of God can originate from things we believe we have done wrong. We can turn away from those actions because we want to be pleasing to the Lord. Concentrating on the sins of the past keeps us in a perpetual struggle to move forward. When we focus on the grace of God, the past will loosen its grip, and we can step into the blessings laid out for us along God's path. Every mistake, every disappointment, every failure is covered by His grace. It is the grace of God that rewrites our stories.

> Sin is no longer your master, for you no longer live under the requirements of the law. Instead, you live under the freedom of God's grace. (Romans 6:14 NLT)

Our Part

People who follow Christ and believe that God hears their prayers have the power of the Holy Spirit to heal broken relationships. We belong to God. When we humbly pray, leaving self-righteousness behind and focusing on the love of Christ, the Holy Spirit empowers us to show His love, joy, and peace to the world. God will always do His part because He is faithful. Can we be faithful followers and do ours?

> If My people who are called by My name will humble themselves, and pray and seek My face, and turn from their wicked ways, then I will hear from heaven, and will forgive their sin and heal their land. Now My eyes will be open and My ears attentive to prayer made in this place. (2 Chronicles 7:14–15 NKJV)

August 31

Abundant Joy

Being in the presence of a positive person can bring feelings of happiness and joy. When we need a course correction, we seek individuals who speak truth and put direction into our lives. Staying in the presence of the Lord will keep the path of His light shining before us. Acknowledging Him in every area of our lives will bring a peace that we don't understand. Even during the toughest of challenges, joy and happiness are abundant in the presence of the Lord.

> You will show me the path to life, abounding joy in your presence, the delights at your right hand forever. (Psalm 16:11 NABRE)

God has restored my life. I once had
nothing, and He gave it all for me.

—DWC graduate

SEPTEMBER

I am a failure.

My road to addiction started when I was nine. I started smoking cigarettes, and I began drinking two years later. When I turned fourteen, I ran away from home so much that I ended up in a juvenile home. I spent the next year and a half of my life in a juvenile home. By age seventeen, I was living on the streets. I stayed with friends, where I started smoking weed and doing pills.

I was twenty years old when I got married the first time. I was able to become clean and sober through my first pregnancy. After having my daughter, the drugs began calling my name. Just days after having my daughter, I was doing speed. I spent my days and nights drinking and partying. Five more years passed, and I found myself in the arms of my second husband with two more baby girls. Being pregnant was the only time I was clean and sober.

After my second divorce, I was high on meth all the time, and I became involved with a man who was also using drugs. We began burglarizing abandoned homes to steal items to pay for drugs. We were ultimately caught, and I went to prison. Even after being locked away from my girls for five years, I didn't learn a thing from being in prison. The week I got out, I started partying again. After two more years, I found myself in yet another failed marriage. All three of my husbands were very abusive in every sense of the word. My children went to live with either their dads or their grandparents.

In 2002, when I was forty-five years old, I was living in Pampa, Texas, and working at United. I had my own apartment. After a life of partying and drinking, the pain became too much for me to bear. On December 28, 2002, the darkness that had been devouring my life and soul overcame me. I remember how dark the nights had become, and even the once-full moon had been reduced to a sliver of its brilliance. It was on this dark night that I decided to end my life. I decided to park my car on the railroad tracks. I didn't want to survive accidentally. I remember sitting there in the darkness, drinking a bottle of whiskey and doing crack.

I knew I was afraid of living, but I was also scared of dying. I was a coward, unable to face the decision to end my life without being drunk and doped up. I sat there for what seemed to be an eternity. The strange thing is, it would have been easy to pray and ask for the train to hurry up and hit me, but for some reason, it was hard to ask God to forgive me and heal me. But God was watching out for me that day. I came to realize, as I silently watched the sunrise in the early dawn, that darkness cannot overcome darkness. If I was to win this fight against the eternal night that had haunted me for so long, I needed to do something different. I needed to bring light to my soul. To do that, I had to be the change. How was it that a train you could set your watch by never came that night? To this day, the only explanation I can come up with is God. He must have been sitting there in the car with me that night. Since I was unable to end my life, I decided I needed to change it. I decided to go back to my mama and daddy's house.

I was done with the drinking and the drugs. I was done with hurting my daddy and mama. I no longer wanted to hurt them by living as an addict. I told my parents that I was an addict, that I couldn't stop using, and that I needed help.

My parents brought me to Amarillo to the Downtown Women's Center Haven House, and I finally got help. Being willing to sit down, shut up, and listen was very hard for me. Learning I was ADD and bipolar and that I had hepatitis C got my attention. I was there for five months and then moved to the Downtown Women's Center Abba House. I was so grateful that DWC accepted me because I believe I wouldn't have made it if they hadn't. I am proud to say that I have been clean and sober since December 31, 2002. Without my parents and DWC, there is no doubt that I would not be here.

I always knew there was a God. I didn't know how much He loved me. Downtown Women's Center taught me the tools I needed to stay clean and sober. I learned to take one day at a time and sometimes one hour or one minute at a time. I learned that my family history of alcoholism was a contributing factor in my struggle. I worked hard and learned to pray and to lean on Jesus.

I work hard to this day and am so proud of myself and grateful to be alive. Thank you to Downtown Women's Center and to my sponsor. Glory be to God!

I am a success.

Hearing His Voice

Sometimes we aren't sure if we are clearly hearing the voice of God. We then become uncertain of moving forward with our next steps. Conversations with mentors and leaders can help, but often, they don't produce the answer. God is always speaking. He communicates to us through people, dreams, nature, music, and a host of other ways. We will hear His voice clearly, and our faith in God will rest on solid ground.

> So then faith comes by hearing, and hearing by the word of God. (Romans 10:17 NKJV)

September 2

A Beautiful Mosaic

A mosaic is a unique and beautiful art form. Tiny pieces, many misshapen or jagged, come together in color, texture, size, and shape to form one beautiful image, held in place by a cement that makes it strong and sturdy. Our lives are like a mosaic—there is not one big thing that totally makes up who we are. A lifetime of decisions, circumstances, relationships, failures, and achievements create the mosaics of our lives. Jesus is the cement that holds us all together. His truth, love, and peace create the beautiful picture that molds us for all the world to see.

> Rejoice in the Lord, O you righteous! For praise from the upright is beautiful. (Psalm 33:1 NKJV)

Seek Me

Have you ever looked through a pair of binoculars to see something but had to adjust the dials and focus in order to see the image clearly?

Our relationship with Jesus often can feel like that. We have to look for His wisdom, which is always found in His Word. When we listen and obey, the Holy Spirit makes the adjustments in our hearts, allowing us to clearly see the image of God. As we diligently search for the Lord, more revelations and right decisions will follow. His love will come into focus and lead us to a deeper understanding of His truth.

> And you will seek Me and find Me, when you search for
> Me with all your heart. (Jeremiah 29:13 NKJV)

September 4

The Same Spirit

Gold does not stay in the refiner's fire. It will spend ages in its intended use or on display but only after being refined—made ready. Spiritually, we are like gold when we go through "the fire" that comes in all of our lives. It is easy to get discouraged when we have negative circumstances in our lives, but we must remember that Jesus lives in us. The same power that raised Him from death to life is alive in us.

Don't be dismayed when circumstances look bleak. Invite Jesus in, and His Holy Spirit will guide you to victory in Him.

> And if the Spirit of him who raised Jesus from the dead is living in you, he who raised Christ from the dead will also give life to your mortal bodies because of his Spirit who lives in you. (Romans 8:11 NIV)

The Perfect Solvent

A pipe, blood vessel, conduit, or river all carry a vital substance from one place to another. Fretting and worrying are both corrosives that can negatively impact our lives. Jesus tells us to trust in Him, have obedience to His leading, and have faith in His promises. As we persevere in applying His remedy to our circumstances, we experience the Holy Spirit flowing through us as the truth of Jesus is carried to our hearts.

> If you love Me, keep My commandments. And I will pray the Father, and He will give you another Helper, that He may abide with you forever—the Spirit of truth, whom the world cannot receive, because it neither sees Him nor knows Him; but you know Him, for He dwells with you and will be in you. I will not leave you orphans; I will come to you. (John 14:15–18 NKJV)

September 6

Hope in the Lord

Have you ever said, "I don't want to get my hopes up too high"?

We usually speak these words because we are fearful of disappointment and that things will not turn out the way we hoped. But do we really want our plans to succeed, or do we want the success of the plans of the One who gives us a future and hope? As we believe in God's promises, we should place our hope in Jesus. Every disappointment will be turned to hope when we allow the Holy Spirit to engage us in His truth.

Keep hope alive in your heart.

> Now hope does not disappoint, because the love of God has been poured out in our hearts by the Holy Spirit who was given to us. (Romans 5:5 NKJV)

He Sees the Best in Us

Seeing potential in others and in ourselves is sometimes difficult. Yet we have no problem with knowing an apple seed can become an apple tree or that a construction site will become a building. The Lord sees the best in us when others might see the worst. And what He sees are not our outward appearances but the seeds of greatness.

> But the Lord said to Samuel: Do not judge from his appearance or from his lofty stature, because I have rejected him. God does not see as a mortal, who sees the appearance. The Lord looks into the heart. (1 Samuel 16:7 NABRE)

September 8

I Am Released

Former prisoners remember the joy and excitement they felt on release day. Those who vow never to go back to bondage make the necessary changes in their lives to stay free.

Jesus died on the cross and set us free. By the power of the Holy Spirit, we are liberated to do what He would do. We are free from worry, free from impure thoughts, and free from striving to be saved. God has released us to serve others, give thanks, tell of His wonderful works, sing praises, be glad, and rejoice. And we never have to be in bondage again!

> Stand fast therefore in the liberty by which Christ has made us free, and do not be entangled again with a yoke of bondage. (Galatians 5:1 NKJV)

Every Day Is a Victory

After the win of a great championship game, athletes wake up the next morning feeling elated about their hard-fought victory. The ups and downs and aches and pains of the past season suddenly become worth it, and the experience of triumph can never be taken away.

Every day of your life is a victory when you have a relationship with Jesus Christ. When you wake up in the morning, learn to develop your thoughts to remember that no matter what comes that day, the true hope is in Jesus Christ!

> So, my dear brothers and sisters, be strong and immovable. Always work enthusiastically for the Lord, for you know that nothing you do for the Lord is ever useless. (1 Corinthians 15:58 NLT)

September 10

Living in His Protection

When we think of enemies, we usually think of those with whom we disagree or someone who has treated us unfairly. Although these adversaries are real, there is an enemy that seeks to destroy our souls and many times attacks our hearts with guilt, anger, greed, jealousy, and a host of other feelings that are not from God. We don't have to fall captive to the enemy's trap. The Lord shows us a better way when we abide in Him. As we focus our passion on God, our conflicts are resolved in Him, and the Holy Spirit will show us how to live in His presence and protection.

> Have mercy on me, my God, have mercy on me, for in you I take refuge. I will take refuge in the shadow of your wings until the disaster has passed. (Psalm 57:1 NIV)

A Life Full of Wisdom

It has been said that we should never question God, but there is a difference between questioning God's ways and asking a question of the Lord. God made us to be curious, and questions constantly run through our minds. Sometimes, where we search for the answer can be an indicator of what we truly believe. It takes faith and discipline to seek wisdom from the Lord first, before we search elsewhere for answers.

If you are searching for wisdom, simply ask Jesus, who was created to be our example of how to live a life full of wisdom. It will be given to you.

> God has united you with Christ Jesus. For our benefit God made him to be wisdom itself. Christ made us right with God; he made us pure and holy, and he freed us from sin. (1 Corinthians 1:30 NLT)

September 12

Complete

There are times when we fail to reach the goals we set for ourselves, such as exercising more, eating healthier, or increasing our prayer time. Beginning a new behavior can be a goal, but changing a pattern of behavior becomes a transformation of our lifestyles. Doing God's work is our goal; therefore, we must change our patterns of behavior by aligning our minds, bodies, and spirits to the Word of God.

> All Scripture is given by inspiration of God, and is profitable for doctrine, for reproof, for correction, for instruction in righteousness, that the man of God may be complete, thoroughly equipped for every good work. (2 Timothy 3:16–17 NKJV)

Harvest Time

For a farmer, harvest is a busy time that requires all hands on deck. It's hard work and labor-intensive, but there is a great reward when the work is done. We always can have an impact on others. Circumstances create the conditions that allow the heart of an individual to be open to receiving God's truth. An encouraging word, an act of generosity, or something as simple as a smile can be the tool that uplifts someone's spirit and gives hope.

Today, as you continue to make prayer a lifestyle, ask God to show you how to achieve the harvest.

> Then He said to them, "The harvest truly is great, but the laborers are few; therefore pray the Lord of the harvest to send out laborers into His harvest." (Luke 10:2 NKJV)

September 14

God's Place

Information and knowledge are abundant in today's world. Anything we want to know is a keystroke away. Many different sources can shape our beliefs, and sometimes we are not sure what the truth is. Uncertainty moves in and takes the place of God's truth. As believers, we can know the truth and not be swayed by false teachings if we are diligent to use the Word of God as our guide.

Don't let anything take the place of God in your heart.

> Children, be on your guard against idols. (1 John 5:21 NABRE)

Special Favor

The Lord's favor is a protection for those who believe in His goodness. It comes with the shield of His love, peace, joy, and comfort. When we walk with the Lord, He guides us with His gracious kindness. When we cast our cares upon Him, trust in His promises, and believe in His Word, special attention is paid to our circumstances, and He blesses us with His favor.

As you walk through this day in the likeness of Jesus Christ, move forward, knowing the Lord's favor will surround and protect you.

> For You, O Lord, will bless the righteous; With favor You will surround him as with a shield. (Psalm 5:12 NKJV)

September 16

A Change in Attitude

From birth to the cross, Jesus had a profound effect on everyone He met. His openness to hearing their stories, the warmth of His love, the humbleness of His character, and His concern for their lives were readily sensed. Was His attitude the invitation to salvation?

Our attitudes toward individuals are detected within seconds of meeting them. Other people instantly gain a sense of how we feel about them. Because we have the mind of Christ, we also can have the attitude of Christ.

Change your attitude to reflect the Lord, and let that be what others see.

> Don't be selfish; don't try to impress others. Be humble, thinking of others as better than yourselves. Don't look out only for your own interests, but take an interest in others, too. You must have the same attitude that Christ Jesus had. (Philippians 2:3–5 NLT)

Just Seek Him

Often in our busy lives, we seek the Lord for guidance, provision, and healing. We want to learn about His ways and His love. When we do, our lives are blessed with His grace and mercy. Seeking the Lord to simply sit in His presence without expectation is a beautiful silence that turns our hearts to adoration. The most powerful love of all is the peaceful love that Jesus pours out on us when we are still.

Slow down, be silent, and open your heart to this love.

> Then Christ will make his home in your hearts as you trust in him. Your roots will grow down into God's love and keep you strong. (Ephesians 3:17 NLT)

September 18

To Listen

God speaks to us in many ways. It is up to us to listen and to act. When Sister Mary Virginia needed money to open DWC, she called her friend. She explained what she was trying to do and that she needed his help. He said, "I was just reading my Bible. The check is in the mail." There was only one condition—that he remain anonymous. On September 18, 1989, the Downtown Women's Center purchased the properties at 405 and 409 South Monroe from Fred Salamy. The Bible verse he was reading?

> Those who shut their ears to the cry of the poor will themselves call out and not be answered. (Proverbs 21:13 NABRE)

I Am Content

Have you ever found yourself at a low time in your life, waiting for the next emotional or physical storm to hit? Maybe you are in a season of abundant overflow, and you recognize that every day is a new blessing from God.

We often focus on the highs and lows that cycle through our lives, allowing circumstances to dictate our faith. Most days, however, we are content; things are okay, and we rest in His peace. Believing in Christ doesn't mean we deny the highs and lows. It simply means that we are making a choice, knowing that everything is going to be OK. We place our trust in Him.

Yet true godliness with contentment is itself great wealth.
(1 Timothy 6:6 NLT)

September 20

Integrity Is Visible

Integrity is visible in the individuals who walk in it. Allowing the Holy Spirit to instruct us while reading the Word of God puts the characteristics of Jesus in our spirits. This draws others to want to know Him. The people who have an impact on our lives hold an unshakable set of values and are known by their honesty, goodness, decency, and love for others. These qualities are the foundation of integrity. When we make the decision to walk in integrity, we are walking in the Spirit of God.

> Joyful are people of integrity, who follow the instructions of the Lord. (Psalm 119:1 NLT)

Pass the Test

We spend much time studying and preparing for a major exam for a class or degree, but stress and anxiety often overshadow our preparations. Faith in God comes with tests that are designed to help us grow as we see His hand in our daily lives. Our faith becomes stronger as we stand firm in knowing that Jesus Christ is who He says He is—our refiner, the purifier, our Savior. When trials lead us to believe we will fail, we remember that faith in God assures us that we have already passed the test!

> In this you rejoice, although now for a little while you may have to suffer through various trials, so that the genuineness of your faith, more precious than gold that is perishable even though tested by fire, may prove to be for praise, glory, and honor at the revelation of Jesus Christ. (1 Peter 1:6–7 NABRE)

September 22

The Power Never Goes Out

Storms can temporarily interrupt electrical power. Suddenly, we experience the loss of the utility that sustains us daily. Sometimes emotional and physical storms in our lives seem to cut us off from our power source. In reality, our power source is never disconnected from us. In fact, if we are rooted in Christ, we will always have the capacity to endure the storm by the power source of the Holy Spirit. The storms in life cannot disrupt the eternal power of God. His mighty power never goes out.

> Finally, draw your strength from the Lord and from his mighty power. (Ephesians 6:10 NABRE)

Trust That Feeling

Call it a hunch, a perception, or intuition. These are all words used to describe something we know in our spirits about a situation or individual. Sometimes, we have a hesitation. Discernment is a gift from the Holy Spirit, and God gives us the ability to know if something is right or wrong.

If you find yourself in a situation where things don't feel right, give yourself permission to trust that feeling and check it out. Trust that the Lord will show you the truth.

> Teach me good judgment and discernment, for I rely on
> your commands. (Psalm 119:66 CSB)

September 24

Greater Works

Healing the sick, giving sight to the blind, and raising the dead to life are just a few of the miracles and wonders that Jesus performed on this earth. The Bible says that when we believe in Him, by the power of the Holy Spirit, we are able to do even greater works than He did. Maybe it is as simple as encouraging individuals that they will make it through their challenges. Could it be helping a neighbor who needs food or financial assistance? The ultimate greater work is sharing our faith in Christ with others.

> See how a person is justified by works and not by faith alone. (James 2:24 NABRE)

To Love the Lost

Sister Mary Virginia shared the gospel with the homeless and listened to their responses to what they heard. She enjoyed hearing their life stories and believed the revelation of Jesus in their individual lives would help them break the chains of homelessness. She received her direction from the Word of God and executed on every word. It was not uncommon for Sister Mary Virginia to literally chase down a woman who was overcome with a desire to leave and love her back to a safe place.

> "What man among you having a hundred sheep and losing one of them would not leave the ninety-nine in the desert and go after the lost one until he finds it? And when he does find it, he sets it on his shoulders with great joy and, upon his arrival home, he calls together his friends and neighbors and says to them, 'Rejoice with me because I have found my lost sheep.' I tell you, in just the same way there will be more joy in heaven over one sinner who repents than over ninety-nine righteous people who have no need of repentance." (Luke 15:4–7 NABRE)

Learn from Me

Being a Christ-follower paves the road to serving others. Jesus becomes the center of everything we know and do. He is our very existence. Jesus shapes our characters and is the foundation of how we influence others. As we learn more about the Lord, we learn more about ourselves, and we are called to make the choice to become more like Jesus. Let's determine in our hearts to allow God's Word to be our primary source of how we live our lives. Let's bless the Lord by living lives that bless others.

> As I learn your righteous regulations, I will thank you by living as I should! (Psalm 119:7 NLT)

His Glorious Image

At some point in time, we all probably have said, "I want to be different," or "I want my life to be better." These words are generally spoken when we face challenges, but we're not certain of what to do. We desire a restart, a new beginning, even a transformation. In order for this to happen, we must understand that the Lord is the one who transforms us for His purposes when we believe in Him. We reflect the glory of God when His light radiates through us, and we are changed.

> So all of us who have had that veil removed can see and reflect the glory of the Lord. And the Lord—who is the Spirit—makes us more and more like him as we are changed into his glorious image. (2 Corinthians 3:18 NLT)

September 28

Use Me

People exist for a purpose, and for the believer in Christ Jesus, that purpose is to be used by God. When we make decisions in life without seeking direction from the Lord, we quietly begin to doubt ourselves. Nobody wants to be used by people, but we do want to be used by God. God will never ask us to do something without His Holy Spirit giving us the power to accomplish it. God has not given us a spirit of fear.

Go ahead and ask the Lord to use you and show you the good works He created for you. You already have been chosen!

> For we are God's masterpiece. He has created us anew in Christ Jesus, so we can do the good things he planned for us long ago. (Ephesians 2:10 NIV)

Eyes Wide Open

When we pray, do we ask the Lord to let us see what He sees and hear what He hears? Praying to be more like Jesus takes enormous courage. As we decide to live completely for the Lord, the Holy Spirit develops a sensitivity in us, enabling us to see and hear as He does. His eyes and ears are open to our emotional, physical, and spiritual struggles. Having the heart of the Lord turns our hearts toward others, and the challenges we face no longer seem paramount. As God's Word saturates our spirits, it opens our eyes to see His wonders.

> But blessed are your eyes because they see, and your ears, because they hear. (Matthew 13:16 NIV)

September 30

Dare to Believe

Our faith in God has to be stretched. Without challenging ourselves to believe God for greater things, our faith may lose its freshness. The Lord desires more for us than we do for ourselves, and when we have faith in God, our hopes and dreams grow exponentially. He is a big God! His will is for us to believe in His majesty, magnificence, and capability to make our dreams come true.

Stretch your faith and dare to believe that God has a plan for your life, a plan that includes your hopes and dreams.

> Now to him who is able to accomplish far more than all we ask or imagine, by the power at work within us, to him be glory in the church and in Christ Jesus to all generations, forever and ever. Amen. (Ephesians 3:20–21 NABRE)

I am worthy of a new beginning.

—DWC graduate

OCTOBER

I am a runner.

I ran from the feeling that I didn't belong. I ran far, far away from the family that called me their own and had given me their name. My adopted parents were at a loss when their dream of raising a beautiful daughter died when she hit the streets. I was doing everything I could to change the way I felt, not realizing that the very thing I needed the most was what I already had—a loving family and a God who saw me no matter where I was.

I started rebelling against all authority and drinking and smoking marijuana at the age of eleven. I ran away from home and had hitchhiked the span of our great United States three times by the time I was fifteen. I found myself in every place I came to, so I would run again. I learned very early in my wanderings that most people on the highway to destruction had no value and no worth, so they would see a young girl hitchhiking as an opportunity to satisfy sick desires.

A way for me to numb the reality that I had become a lady of assignation was to do drugs—and a lot of them. My loving parents had signed their rights over to the state, and I was truly without anyone to care for me but the lonely men on dark roads to nowhere. I bounced, always chasing shadows, from one state to another, one facility to another, and even ran away from a foster home back to the streets that consumed me. I didn't know what to do with myself and the emotions that came from my drifting soul, so I started cutting myself so badly that I ended up in hospitals and mental institutions. I was institutionalized in the cobweb that stretched out in the corner of my dark mind.

After a brief stint in a California jail, after being arrested on drug trafficking charges, I lost even more of myself to the abyss and began shooting drugs into my already deeply scarred arms, just to forget about the wounds to my heart. Somehow, in the middle of this war, I gave birth to a son who bears the scars of my regretful choices, even now, as an adult. Two more children came in a moment of sobriety, but when addiction came back full circle, I ran again, giving them all away to be raised by the same parents I had left behind.

Losing things became a new way of life. I lost homes, cars, jobs, and my body, all in an effort to get the next high. I was lost, disassociating myself from every feeling I had when doing whatever needed to be done to forget.

Somehow, I found myself stepping across the threshold of the Downtown Women's Center and right into the arms of Sister Mary Virginia. That beautiful saint of a woman had no problem chasing me down the street when I would run away to the dope dealer fronting as a body shop owner a few blocks away. Playing pretense was not my forte. What ensued were years of jails, institutions, and near death, riddled with short periods of sobriety. The cutting seemed to be the only way to manage my inward pain in an outward expression based solely on fear.

My darkest day was when I accepted my own death while being held hostage by a raging man with eyes as dark as a starless night. I never thought my life would end that way, but I was on my knees in front of a man who was about to kill me. I believe God stepped into the madness emerging from the very pores of this evil man, and I was able to live that day and not die. Prison came again, and I realized I was safe—from the drugs, from death, and from myself. My reasoning took a turn from institutionalization toward a freedom I couldn't fathom, especially sitting in a jail cell.

I had life figured out, or so I thought, until October 3, 2005, when I finally surrendered to a program of recovery and a God of my understanding. I ultimately stopped running from things that did not satisfy me and started running toward a life I didn't know I could have.

I believe that my last trip to prison was the wake-up call I needed because I was hemmed in on all sides and forced to silently contemplate my existence and how God had saved me from certain death more than once. On my last trip to the Downtown Women's Center, I was able to piece together all the times in my life when I was shown love by people who cared for me, even when I was unlovable. The people at the Downtown Women's Center desired life for me more than I desired life for myself, so I succumbed. I took baby steps toward a loving God when this dead woman walking lonely streets walked right into the arms of the One who saves.

I am more than a conqueror!

Redeemed

After winning a lottery, you redeem the ticket for the reward. The amount won may determine your level of happiness. If it is a large amount, every joyous emotion may burst to the surface in your heart because you know your life has changed forever.

Every day that God gives us breath can be filled with that same joy because He has redeemed us from sin and death. There was a joy set before Jesus as He endured the cross, knowing our salvation was His reward. Our redemption at the cross can be celebrated because we know we are set for eternity.

> In Him we have redemption through His blood, the forgiveness of sins, according to the riches of His grace which He made to abound toward us in all wisdom and prudence. (Ephesians 1:7–8 NKJV)

The Lifter of My Head

Broken, hopeless, and homeless was her condition as she walked into a Bible study in a homeless shelter, nine hundred miles from home. The weight of thirty years of addiction, shame, and embarrassment wouldn't allow her to look up and make eye contact. She didn't think anything or anyone could change her situation. She was wrong. As she listened to the story of the woman at the well in John 4, she started to find hope. She found Jesus—the lifter of her head. Seventeen years clean, unashamed, and victorious, she now knows the Lord heard her cries.

He hears yours too.

> But You, O Lord, are a shield for me, My glory and the One who lifts up my head. I cried to the Lord with my voice, and He heard me from His holy hill. (Psalm 3:3–4 NKJV)

Cheerful Giver

The kingdom principle of giving is that God gives it back to us, pressed down, shaken together, and overflowing with abundance. With joy and delight, the Lord gives liberally to us everything we need. As we pray to have the heart of the Lord, the joy of giving is infused inside our beings. Generosity becomes a lifestyle and a permanent part of who we are. The Holy Spirit creates a joy in us that cannot be contained when we search for opportunities to meet the needs of others. God loves when we give with overwhelming joy.

> Each of you should give what you have decided in your heart to give, not reluctantly or under compulsion, for God loves a cheerful giver. And God is able to bless you abundantly, so that in all things at all times, having all that you need, you will abound in every good work. (2 Corinthians 9:7–8 NIV)

October 4

Sensitivity to His Voice

Words can sometimes be designed to desensitize and make us receptive to a narrative that is not true. Our beliefs, self-esteem, and characters are shaped by a lifetime of words. Our spirits respond to what we hear. What voice do we want to hear? The Holy Spirit will help us develop a sensitivity to the tender, loving voice of the Lord, who always speaks truth and directs us in the way we should go. As we read and hear God's Word, we pray for a sensitivity to His voice and to know His love, kindness, and truth.

> Cause me to hear Your lovingkindness in the morning,
> For in You do I trust; Cause me to know the way in which
> I should walk, For I lift up my soul to You. (Psalm 143:8
> NKJV)

Things Above

When you awaken each morning, what are your first thoughts? You may not be able to control the circumstances of the day, but you can decide what you set your mind upon. The Bible says to think on things above, and you must determine for yourself what that means. As you pray today, keep your mind away from how you are going to fix things, and cast your cares on Jesus. Every time you think about the Lord, you are thinking on the things above.

> If then you were raised with Christ, seek those things which are above, where Christ is, sitting at the right hand of God. Set your mind on things above, not on things on the earth. (Colossians 3:1–2 NKJV)

October 6

All Things Are Possible

In order for track runners to place in a meet, it is understood that they must run and stay on the track. The field creates the boundaries, but there are no limits to how fast they can run to accomplish amazing feats. It is easy to find an excuse for why we can't do something, but sometimes, we need to look for reasons why we can. There are boundaries in life, but there are no limits in Christ. We can accomplish the impossible. As followers of Jesus Christ, the Word of God is the field we run on, and our faith in God determines how high we soar.

> But Jesus looked at them and said, "With men it is impossible, but not with God; for with God all things are possible." (Mark 10:27 NKJV)

Walk the Path with Jesus

An employer noticed an employee who was always joyful. Curiously, he asked her why she was so happy all the time. She responded, "Because I have Jesus. I don't know what I would do without Him."

Walking this life with Jesus will produce the ability to be more like Him, and joy is always the outcome. As you pray, believe in the Word of God and His purpose that is planted in your heart. Walk with Jesus along the path of life so that others will be drawn to Him.

> You will show me the path of life; in Your presence is fullness of joy; At Your right hand are pleasures forevermore. (Psalm 16:11 NKJV)

October 8

One Body, One Mission

The concept of teamwork is biblical. In the Old Testament, Moses's father-in-law encouraged him to gather a team to assist with leading and governing the children of Israel. In the New Testament, we are called to be members of the body of Christ, with the job assignment of spreading the good news. God has given us a great assignment, but we don't have to do it alone. We just have to do our part. When we join together with a similar purpose and love for each other, our mission will be completed.

> For as the body is one and has many members, but all the members of that one body, being many, are one body, so also *is* Christ. (1 Corinthians 12:12 NKJV)

Just Takes a Little Faith

Sometimes in life, we encounter emotional or physical giants that seem impossible to defeat. Time is spent worrying about the situation, and before we know it, our beliefs about the issue don't line up with the truth. At times, we want God to remove the mountain, but He wants us to know we can scale it. The Holy Spirit gives us the strength to conquer whatever is put before us. It just takes a little faith in Jesus to move that mountain!

> So Jesus said to them, "Because of your unbelief; for assuredly, I say to you, if you have faith as a mustard seed, you will say to this mountain, 'Move from here to there,' and it will move; and nothing will be impossible for you." (Matthew 17:20 NKJV)

What Do You Have in Your Hands?

There are people who have the ability to see the value of an item that others see as trash. Old cars and damaged furniture may be turned into a work of art. In the right hands, items become invaluable. In Exodus 4, what Moses thought was just a rod turned out to be the power of God in his hands, and he used it so people would believe. As followers of Jesus, we have the power of God in our hands—the Holy Spirit!

As you pray, ask the Holy Spirit to use you in a way that is pleasing to the Lord so that others will come to know God.

> He raises the needy from the dust; from the ash heap lifts up the poor, To seat them with nobles and make a glorious throne their heritage. "For the pillars of the earth are the Lord's, and he has set the world upon them." (1 Samuel 2:8 NABRE)

The Lord Can See the Way

After months of being at home, a couple packed and took off on a road trip. As they made their way to the interstate, visibility was obscured by a thick layer of fog. They exited and waited at a truck stop for the fog to lift, but time ticked on. The semitrucks kept moving, so they decided that maybe the truckers knew something they didn't. Cautiously, they followed the trucks, and after a few miles, the sky was clear.

Sometimes, we just need to follow someone who has more information than we do. When we can't see our way, know that the Lord can.

> Your ears shall hear a word behind you, saying, "This is the way, walk in it," Whenever you turn to the right hand Or whenever you turn to the left. (Isaiah 30:21 NKJV)

October 12

Fellowship with Christ

There are places on earth that contain beauty and calmness, and all we want to do is stay there. Whether it is looking out over the vastness of the ocean, the majestic mountains, or the delicate grace of a field of lilies, our minds go to the place where perfect peace makes us feel alive. The presence of the Lord is a place where we can remain, and when we do, His love creates in us an eternal hope of peace. We can choose to live there every day.

As you pray, ask the Holy Spirit to help you remain in fellowship with Christ; this is your home of perfect peace.

> Your eyes will see the king in his beauty and view a land that stretches afar. (Isaiah 33:17)

Never Alone

When you feel lonely, do you recognize that you are never alone and that there is a loving presence constantly with you? In fact, that presence has always been in your life and is the same yesterday, today, and forever. God has made you a promise to always be with you. As you pray, ask the Holy Spirit to increase your awareness and understanding that the One who made you loves you, and He will always be with you.

> I will be your God throughout your lifetime—until your hair is white with age. I made you, and I will care for you. I will carry you along and save you. (Isaiah 46:4 NLT)

October 14

Practice Makes Better

Professional athletic teams spend months in training, preparing for the opening game. Skills are practiced in an effort to be flawless on game day. The game is rarely without error. Practice is continued, and the team gets better. What if we adopted a mindset like professional athletes and practiced glorifying the Lord every day? What if, happy or sad, glorifying the Lord became our daily purpose?

As you pray, ask the Holy Spirit to remind you to practice giving glory to the Lord. His love is everlasting!

> Because your love is better than life, my lips will glorify you. (Psalm 63:3 NIV)

Step Toward It

What is holding you back from stepping into the purpose that God has set for your life? Is it a lie you have been told, fear, procrastination, unbelief, uncertainty, or all the above?

Every day, we make decisions that set the direction for our lives. Holding on to past mistakes and failures is a decision that can lead our hearts to carry bitterness. Looking forward to the future helps to inspire us to press on. The present is filled with the hope that fuels our hearts with strength. The decisions we make in the present are the decisions God uses to bring about our future.

> A man's heart plans his way, But the Lord directs his steps.
> (Proverbs 16:9 NKJV)

October 16

Joy

Today, let's start the day with joy because the joy of the Lord is our strength, and those we serve need to be reassured by our steadiness. Together, we can do it!

> These things I have spoken to you, that My joy may remain in you, and that your joy may be full. (John 15:11 NKJV)

Living in the Shadow

Living in the shadow of God is living in the image of God. It is so comfortable to sit in the shade on a hot summer day. You feel the warmth of the sun, but within the shadow of a tree, you feel peaceful rest. The shade is God's shadow, and He is always available to us.

Take time to sit in the shade.

> You indeed are my savior, and in the shadow of your wings
> I shout for joy. (Psalm 63:8 NABRE)

October 18

The Spirit Is in the Chaos

Sometimes, when there seems to be a lot of chaos in our lives, God is actually giving us time to sort things out. During this chaotic period, God has redeemed us. What a beautiful gift we have been given!

Take time to reflect on what God has brought you through. Meditate on the things that are pure, just, and honorable. Believe that this is your season to strengthen your purpose and that the Holy Spirit is in the chaos.

> Jesus answered and said to him, "What I am doing, you
> do not understand now, but you will understand later."
> (John 13:7 NABRE)

Look Straight Ahead

Sometimes when we reflect on past events in our lives, it has a way of holding us captive to things we cannot change. The better choices we make today will lead to a better life tomorrow. The question, then, becomes, are we living attached to the past or stepping into the future? We are not bound by what was; we are free to walk the path of what can be.

As you pray today, ask the Holy Spirit to release you from what was and show you what can be, through thoughtful and planned choices.

> Let your eyes look straight ahead; fix your gaze directly before you. Give careful thought to the paths for your feet and be steadfast in all your ways. (Proverbs 4:25–26 NIV)

Always and Forever

The concept of eternity can be hard to understand because we are so driven by time. The human mind dissects activities in segments, knowing that an event, a task, or the day will eventually come to an end.

God is not bound by time. In your prayer time, ask the Holy Spirit to show you the depth and meaning of eternity, forever, always—words God uses to describe His love for you.

> Yet God has made everything beautiful for its own time. He has planted eternity in the human heart, but even so, people cannot see the whole scope of God's work from beginning to end. So I concluded there is nothing better than to be happy and enjoy ourselves as long as we can. (Ecclesiastes 3:11–12 NLT)

The Main Thing

Sometimes when we see success in others, it is common to think they have easy lives. A closer examination of their lives, however, reveals that time was spent in the valley of discouragement and on the mountaintop of glory. Human struggles and victories are recorded throughout history, and no one is immune. The main thing for believers to remember is that the Lord is with us through good and bad times. The Lord holds us up when we think we can't go another step.

As you pray, thank the Lord for His constant love and presence, as He is the One who is always with you.

> May the Lord our God be with us as he was with our ancestors; may he never leave us or abandon us. May he give us the desire to do his will in everything and to obey all the commands, decrees, and regulations that he gave our ancestors. (1 Kings 8:57–58 NLT)

October 22

Worship in Holiness

Have you ever been grateful to people for something they did for you, but you didn't know how to thank them? You probably knew their incredible act of generosity was born out of love for you.

Jesus went to the cross so that we could be saved from sin and death. He didn't require anything from us beforehand. Jesus gave it all from His purest of love for us.

As you pray, give the Lord the glory and honor He is due for the great and small things He has done. Ask the Holy Spirit to teach you how to worship the Lord in holiness.

> Give unto the Lord, O you mighty ones, Give unto the Lord glory and strength. Give unto the Lord the glory due to His name; Worship the Lord in the beauty of holiness. (Psalm 29:1–2 NKJV)

Two Are Better than One

A woman was asked to serve in a ministry role involving young children. It wasn't new to her, but it had been a while since she had experienced the environment that twenty rambunctious kiddos can create. She did the only thing she knew to do; she called her best friend for help.

God never meant for us to go it alone. He created friendship. Serving others with someone we trust brings a joy and comfort that cannot be explained. When we cultivate and nurture our relationships, over time, everlasting love and respect are the rewards.

> Two are better than one, Because they have a good reward for their labor. For if they fall, one will lift up his companion. But woe to him who is alone when he falls, For he has no one to help him up. (Ecclesiastes 4:9–10 NKJV)

October 24

His Righteousness

Saying yes to Jesus begins the process of becoming the righteousness of Christ. It is a gift from God to be righteous, which is a conscious decision to live life as Jesus lived. As believers, we represent Jesus Christ to the world, and to some, we are the only Jesus they will ever see. Our only desire should be for the world to see us clothed in His righteousness.

> Now then, we are ambassadors for Christ, as though God were pleading through us: we implore you on Christ's behalf, be reconciled to God. For He made Him who knew no sin to be sin for us, that we might become the righteousness of God in Him. (2 Corinthians 5:20–21 NKJV)

Journey of Love

Have you given much thought to what it means to pray?

Sometimes, prayer can feel like something that has to be done in order to complete a transaction with God, to move Him to do what we want. A beautiful exchange takes place in prayer when we remove the pressure of believing it is something we have to do. God has not limited us to how we pray to Him, and there are many ways to seek the Lord. When we pray, let it be an amazing journey of love with God, our Father.

> Sing to Him, sing psalms to Him; Talk of all His wondrous works! Glory in His holy name; Let the hearts of those rejoice who seek the Lord! Seek the Lord and His strength; Seek His face evermore! (Psalm 105:2–4 NKJV)

October 26

Strength to Endure

If we are driving in an ice storm and the car begins to slide, we take our foot off the gas and follow the skid without applying the brake to stop the car from sliding. It may take a few times before we get the hang of it because turning a steering wheel into the slide is not natural.

Rejoicing in the Lord during challenging times does not make sense either. When you pray, praise the Lord in good times and in bad. You can rest in knowing the Holy Spirit is infusing you with the strength to endure until the "storm" is over.

> We can rejoice, too, when we run into problems and trials, for we know that they help us develop endurance. (Romans 5:3 NLT)

Have No Anxiety

When is the last time you knew true peace—the peace that soothes thought, where anxiety and stress are lowered? Peace has been brought to you by the Father, the true peace. Today, allow the Holy Spirit to fill your mind and spirit with the peace that comes from the Lord. It is His peace that will give you a place to stand and live amid all the unknowns around you.

> Have no anxiety at all, but in everything, by prayer and petition, with thanksgiving, make your requests known to God. (Philippians 4:6 NABRE)

October 28

Unwavering Faith

Believing and trusting in God is a core belief of the followers of Jesus Christ. Can we wake up every morning with the certainty of knowing the day will be filled with hope and blessings? Is it possible to have unwavering faith, believing fully that God has a plan for our lives?

Greet each morning and end each evening with these beliefs and faith. Your life will be different, fuller, more satisfying.

> Therefore I say to you, whatever things you ask when you pray, believe that you receive them, and you will have them. (Mark 11:24 NKJV)

Ask in My Name

A teenager asked her parents for an expensive gift for her birthday. Her parents stretched their monthly dollars and gave their daughter her gift. There can be a gap between the asking and being accepting of what happens next. There are parts of our lives that only God can repair or answer through His love.

Continue your prayers, even bold ones. Be patient. Be accepting. Live with faith in the goodness of God.

> And whatever you ask in My name, that I will do, that the Father may be glorified in the Son. If you ask anything in My name, I will do it. (John 14:13–14 NKJV)

Through Our Faith

Sometimes we get tired. We have challenges, some as big as mountains. Staying in the moment and doing the next right thing is important. It is important that we stay close to God's heart as we regain energy to live the full life of faith. We take that faith into our health, relationships, jobs, money, and children. God can make our mountains into calm valleys. Step out. Step forward.

> For every child of God defeats this evil world, and we achieve this victory through our faith. (1 John 5:4 NLT)

Temptation

Temptation is something we all know about. Maybe temptation is giving into fast food. Perhaps we spend hard-earned dollars but not in the best way. Social media can tempt us to post something we now regret. God's strength in us is stronger and greater than the temptation that is pulling on us. We can walk with the smile of faith as we turn aside from the temptation to the fulfillment of a life of faith.

> No temptation has overtaken you except such as is common to man; but God is faithful, who will not allow you to be tempted beyond what you are able, but with the temptation will also make the way of escape, that you may be able to bear it. (1 Corinthians 10:13 NKJV)

I felt lost my whole life, but when I came to DWC, I learned who I am. I am a daughter of the Most High King.

—DWC graduate

NOVEMBER

I am a junkie.

When I was twelve years old, I started smoking pot, which led to pills, and before long, I experimented with Ecstasy. I was partying and raving all the time, and at sixteen, I started using meth. I got into a relationship with a drug addict who was hooked on OxyContin, so I took full advantage of that. When our relationship ended, I had no means to get pills, so I started using heroin. I was on heroin for more than three years. I knew it would kill me if I didn't stop, and the only way I knew how to do that was to start shooting meth into my tiny veins. Jails, institutions, and death, oh my.

I had racked up one felony charge after another and was literally on the run when I found out I was pregnant with my daughter. In a desperate effort to save not only my life but also that of my unborn child, my mom decided to turn me in. That's when I found myself behind bars. I thank my mom for that because I haven't turned back since then. I have two children now and have been clean for more than three years.

I can't pinpoint why I started using drugs and ponder it daily. My dad is an addict and was never around for me as a child. When I was in the seventh grade, I would let him crawl through my window to sleep off his high because I loved him too much to let him be on the streets as a homeless vagabond. I would sneak breakfast to him in the mornings so that he would stay safe in my room, and by the time I made it back from the kitchen, used needles would already be lying on my bed. There is never a time when I haven't known my dad to be high. Eventually, I became my dad's buddy. We helped each other get high by sticking needles in each other's arms. I even stooped to selling drugs to try to keep him off the streets. He became abusive at times. Regardless, I loved him more than my own life. He is still so very lost in his addiction. I am unsure if I will ever see him draw a clean breath.

My mom was a single mom of four. Most days, she was depressed and wouldn't get out of bed, though she did try with all her might to find herself in the chaos of her life. I guess I had no real chance of a clean and sober life because of the cards already on the table that created my destiny.

The Downtown Women's Center was my only option when I came out of jail. I found out about it from a girl in my cell. The DWC saved my life in more ways than I can speak. Having their support when I was lonely and lost was life-changing for me.

I first took notice of God in my childhood. My mom would try to get us to the church between her three jobs. My nanny had given me my first Bible when I was a little girl. I knew I had a connection with God and prayed to Him daily. God would speak to me as a teen when I started drifting into groups of peers that did not have my best interest at heart, and I always felt guilty for not listening to the voice that told me, "This is the way. Walk in it."

When I was sixteen and using meth, I cried out to the Lord to help me, but I felt Him disappearing from my life a little more every day. I know He never left me; I fled Him. In the middle of one of my darkest times, I knew God touched me. I was sitting in the garage with the door open as rain pounded down in sheets on the pavement. I talked to Him and begged Him to show me that He was still with me. I looked up in the clouds at that very moment and saw a hand reaching out for me. I lined my hand up with the mighty hand of God in the clouds and felt a warmth come over me, as if I was being covered in shimmering gold.

Even when I lost myself, God always knew where I'd left me. He came for me and set me free.

Every day, I thank the Lord for seeing me for who I am in Him and not who the world says I am. Today, I am in church every time the doors open, raising my children in the best environment on earth.

I am healed!

November 1

The Rock

What do you think of when you hear the word *rock*? Some might think of Dwayne Johnson; others might think of the Rocky Mountains. Whatever your image, the word *rock* can mean power, strength, longevity, and even beauty. The word can also describe a follower of Jesus. If you feel weak, fearful, or not good enough, remember that your faith has a solid foundation. Step out with faith in your daily walk with God.

> He is the Rock, His work is perfect; For all His ways are justice, A God of truth and without injustice; Righteous and upright is He. (Deuteronomy 32:4 NKJV)

He Has the Answer

After a meeting, two friends decided to have a late lunch to catch up and share about their lives. Conversation was fun and enjoyable. When their lunch was finished, they were surprised to learn that a friend had paid for their meal.

As Christ's followers, sometimes we become lost in our challenges. While we are seeking an answer, God has already sent His solution. When was the last time you were surprised by God's goodness?

> But as for me, Lord, my prayer to you is for a time of favor. In your abundant, faithful love, God, answer me with your sure salvation. (Psalm 69:13 CSB)

November 3

The Heart behind the Answer

Casual interactions and pleasantries take place every day at work, with friends, or with families. When the Christ-follower yields to the power of the Holy Spirit, even the most common encounters can ignite the spark of renewal.

When you ask questions or say hello to others, you will see the heart behind their answers. You and your expression of faith offer the fruit of hope and encouragement.

> And this I pray, that your love may abound still more and more in knowledge and all discernment, that you may approve the things that are excellent, that you may be sincere and without offense till the day of Christ, being filled with the fruits of righteousness which are by Jesus Christ, to the glory and praise of God. (Philippians 1:9–11 NKJV)

A Beautiful Exchange

Prayer is the beautiful exchange we have with our Father. As praise and worship are given to the Lord in prayer, He gives us power to endure. What if we added the following three questions to our prayers: How can I fully love others? How can I give a blessing to someone today? How can I live a daily life of faith? God's answers will give us blessings of our own.

> Bless the Lord, O my soul; And all that is within me, bless His holy name! (Psalm 103:1 NKJV)

November 5

Coming In and Going Out

As we go through our daily lives, sometimes frustration or weariness overwhelms us. From time to time, Jesus rested and withdrew from His disciples. Jesus knew He needed to go away to recharge—these were "breathers with God."

Take your own moments to withdraw and renew your joy and connection to the Lord. This pattern of coming in and going out is a demonstration of spiritual strength and wisdom.

But Jesus often withdrew to the wilderness for prayer.
(Luke 5:16 NLT)

Chosen

Children will sometimes play games where they pick team captains, and then individuals are chosen by the captain. If you have ever played in such a game, you know to wait for your name to be called. As a follower of Christ, you have already been chosen by our true captain. Let your identity be wrapped up in Jesus, and His marvelous light will shine for all to see.

> But you are a chosen generation, a royal priesthood, a holy nation, His own special people, that you may proclaim the praises of Him who called you out of darkness into His marvelous light; who once were not a people but are now the people of God, who had not obtained mercy but now have obtained mercy. (1 Peter 2:9–10 NKJV)

Love Offering

There are times when we treat our belief in God as a list. Prayer, church, and service may start out as an act of love, but often, it can become a duty. As Christ's followers, we must guard against going through the motions and becoming stale. His love for us will never grow stale.

Find a body of believers to serve, and fellowship with them out of love for God's people. Let your gifts be a love offering to the Lord.

> We love Him because He first loved us. (1 John 4:19 NKJV)

Know the Truth

A good detective story has a lot of twists and turns. What looks true about a situation may end up not being true at all. Rest assured that Jesus continues to pray for us. By staying connected to Him, hearing His voice through the Word of God, and by the Holy Spirit, we have the ability to know and walk in truth.

> Make them holy by your truth; teach them your word, which is truth. (John 17:17 NLT)

November 9

Free My Mind

We create prisons in our minds that seem unbreakable. Shackles are placed on the way we think, and our emotions confine us to believing there is no way out. That simply is not true! God sent His Son, Jesus, to break every chain that binds us. Believing in Him gives us the power to free our minds of everything other than His truth. Jesus has set us free, and it is up to us to stay free by living a life acceptable to the Lord.

Pray that the Holy Spirit will free our minds to believe the truth of Jesus Christ.

> The Spirit of the Lord is upon me, because he has anointed me to bring glad tidings to the poor. He has sent me to proclaim liberty to captives and recovery of sight to the blind, to let the oppressed go free, and to proclaim a year acceptable to the Lord. (Luke 4:18–19 NABRE)

Waiting Expectantly

Waiting is a common experience at some point in our lives. We come prepared to wait at the doctor's office, the grocery store, or in traffic. Why, then, is it so hard to patiently wait for the answers to our prayers?

Learn to humbly wait with bold expectations, and listen for guidance from a God who loves you and all those in your world.

> O Lord, hear me as I pray; pay attention to my groaning. Listen to my cry for help, my King and my God, for I pray to no one but you. Listen to my voice in the morning, Lord. Each morning I bring my requests to you and wait expectantly. (Psalm 5:1–3 NLT)

November 11

Good Intentions

There are times when we want to make a change in our lives. We put things off, telling ourselves we will do it tomorrow. Good intentions, however, do not create change. While we are waiting on God, He is waiting on us. When we move, He moves. There is a sweet connection alive in us that pushes us to turn our good intentions into right decisions.

> For God is working in you, giving you the desire and the power to do what pleases him. (Philippians 2:13 NLT)

Come to Me

When we visit with neighbors or family, we may take on more problems than we can easily help resolve. Through the Holy Spirit, we can love and comfort those around us and give encouragement too. Jesus promised to give us problem-solving abilities. If we will simply come to Him with our burdens, God promises to always respond.

> Then Jesus said, "Come to me, all of you who are weary and carry heavy burdens, and I will give you rest." (Matthew 11:28 NLT)

Hear the Quieter Power

Each day, there are sounds all around us. The ongoing traffic, neighbors, and our own family will replace the early morning silence. Mixed in with these sounds is the quieter power of the Holy Spirit, leading Christ-followers to live a life of faith. When our thoughts line up with the Word of God, we know how important it is to balance the sounds and the noise with God's sound. Let the words of the Lord be the sound we hear above all others.

Give ear and hear my voice, pay attention and hear my word: (Isaiah 28:23 NABRE)

Optimistic Joy

There are too many refugee camps in too many places around the world. They become home to too many families and especially children, for years. Optimism is hard to maintain when everything around you seems without hope. Yet children do learn that families can eat around a cookstove, affirming their love for each other.

We are to remain faithful in the staying power of Christ to be present in their lives as they worship, say their own prayers, and believe in the tomorrow to come.

> Dear friends, don't be surprised at the fiery trials you are going through, as if something strange were happening to you. Instead, be very glad—for these trials make you partners with Christ in his suffering, so that you will have the wonderful joy of seeing his glory when it is revealed to all the world. (1 Peter 4:12–13 NLT)

November 15

Divine Silence

Untangling a necklace or earbuds can frustrate even the most patient of us. Sometimes, it's the same with another person's worries or anxieties. We do our best listening and "untangling" that we can, but we will leave the untangling to His wisdom, staying close by as answers come and the tangles of life are straightened.

> He was oppressed and treated harshly, yet he never said a word. He was led like a lamb to the slaughter. And as a sheep is silent before the shearers, he did not open his mouth. (Isaiah 53:7 NLT)

God Is Always Pursuing

Even as Christ-followers, we have a habit of doing things on our own strength and timing. The Word of God tells us to support those with material or financial needs and to tell a friend about God's goodness, even when we are unsure ourselves. Our strength and timing come from Him, and when matched to His gifts, the results are amazing.

Trust the God in you, and go forward.

> Where can I go to escape your Spirit? Where can I flee from your presence? If I go up to heaven, you are there; if I make my bed in Sheol, you are there. (Psalm 139:7–8 CSB)

Obedience Is Better than Sacrifice

Many times, we go our own ways, mistakenly thinking of the sacrifice we are making. Of course, this gets us out of sync with God. He loves us unconditionally, and His direction for our lives is for our good, not His. He knows fully; we only know in part, allowing the Holy Spirit to lead us on the true path—His path.

> But Samuel replied, "What is more pleasing to the Lord: your burnt offerings and sacrifices or your obedience to his voice? Listen! Obedience is better than sacrifice, and submission is better than offering the fat of rams." (1 Samuel 15:22 NLT)

A Life of Faith

A belief system is a pattern of thinking that is developed over time. Our environment, the set of values we live by, and family shape our beliefs. But have we stopped to consider that the things we do and say may either grow or limit the faith of others?

As you pray, ask the Lord to make you a follower who shows those around His trust and His way to a full life of faith.

> Beware of false prophets who come disguised as harmless sheep but are really vicious wolves. You can identify them by their fruit, that is, by the way they act. Can you pick grapes from thornbushes, or figs from thistles? A good tree produces good fruit, and a bad tree produces bad fruit. (Matthew 7:15–17 NLT)

Love That Supersedes

As Christ-followers, we may have differences of opinion about worship, children, politics, or cultural beliefs. God is active and present in all of these. Our active faith will turn down the temperature of any argument. We may walk away disagreeing, but our love for Jesus will remind us of our love for each other. His love never goes away, always providing support and guidance.

> Remind everyone about these things, and command them in God's presence to stop fighting over words. Such arguments are useless, and they can ruin those who hear them. (2 Timothy 2:14 NLT)

Dream and Plan Diligently

Everyone has dreams. Maybe yours include having a family, getting a new job, or walking across the stage with your degree. Do not set your dreams and hopes aside. Prepare yourself for fulfilled dreams by studying, seeking support from family and friends, and having the faith in yourself and in God's plan to dream, to hope, to act. Being successful in faith is a right and true dream.

> Blessed is the one who endures trials, because when he has stood the test he will receive the crown of life that God has promised to those who love him. (James 1:12 CSB)

How We Overcome

Every day, we face spiritual challenges, big or small, new or old. We are at our best when we recall past challenges and claim the gift God has given us to meet our challenges and the grace to recognize that no one faces everything alone. The teachings of others add to our wisdom and spiritual power. With God's presence beside us, overcoming will be our outcome.

> Put on the full armor of God so that you can stand against
> the schemes of the devil. (Ephesians 6:11 CSB)

Spiritual Healing

When our bodies get out of rhythm, doctors use medication or medical procedures to restore them. Our spiritual health can get out of rhythm and balance as well. Taking responsibility for our spiritual conditions will improve our relationships with the Lord. Healing can come from simple things, such as relying on the richness of the Word, talking with spiritual friends, and exercising to break up what we hold on to. Living and working with a healthy balance feels good and is good.

> Get rid of all bitterness, rage, anger, harsh words, and slander, as well as all types of evil behavior. Instead, be kind to each other, tenderhearted, forgiving one another, just as God through Christ has forgiven you. (Ephesians 4:31–32 NLT)

Storm or Calm

Unsettling weather events can create physical damage and feelings of not being safe. Afterward, when calm replaces the storm, safety returns. The Word of God tells us to stay close to Him and know His peace, even in the midst of unsettling weather. The "storm" could be at work or with family.

Mountain or valley, storm or calm, God is there, present with you through it all. You are not alone.

> This is what the Sovereign Lord, the Holy One of Israel, says: "Only in returning to me and resting in me will you be saved. In quietness and confidence is your strength. But you would have none of it." (Isaiah 30:15 NLT)

Safe and Secure

Everyone desires to feel safe. We purchase security systems, park in lighted areas, and leave work with friends. We seek relationship stability in self-help books, therapy, and exercising. Not any one action is enough. In the same way, prayer alone is not enough. We need to study and worship with others, along with consistency in our spiritual practice. We are then surrounded in our faith and feel secure and safe.

> But whoever listens to me will dwell safely, And will be secure, without fear of evil. (Proverbs 1:33 NKJV)

Thankful for Jesus

We have been blessed by God in abundance! We have many reasons to be thankful. When we pray our thanks, we remember the gifts of the Spirit, the same gifts we share freely with others. Blessings are not ours to keep from the lives of others.

> Enter into His gates with thanksgiving, And into His courts with praise. Be thankful to Him, and bless His name. For the Lord is good; His mercy is everlasting, And His truth endures to all generations. (Psalm 100:4–5 NKJV)

Short-Term Memory Loss

As believers, we know that living in the presence of the Lord is the true peace. There are times, however, when we live out old sins—ways that move us away from God. When we remember what really works best for us, we should not be surprised that God's peace never moved, and the temporary separation was just short-term memory loss.

Enjoy your life by living in the now of today, always with Him.

> Yet when you seek the Lord, your God, from there, you shall indeed find him if you search after him with all your heart and soul. (Deuteronomy 4:29 NABRE)

God Does Not Keep Score

If God kept a scorecard of all the things you have done or tried to do, what would be your score?

The good news is that our successes and our failures do not show on God's scorecard. His love surrounds us, goes before us, and stands beside us at all times. We need no other coach.

> We know how much God loves us, and we have put our
> trust in his love. God is love, and all who live in love live
> in God, and God lives in them. (1 John 4:16 NLT)

Inseparable

Every day, the Lord nourishes our hearts with His love. The love Jesus has for us is inseparable from the love of the Father. It is a great, sustaining love. We can open our hearts to believing and receiving the one thing that joins us to the Father—the love of Jesus Christ.

> I have loved you even as the Father has loved me. Remain in my love. (John 15:9 NLT)

November 29

Ambitious Faith

Ambition is a quality admired by many. The drive and desire to be the best at whatever we do can be the catalyst for success. It should be our daily prayer to have such ambitious faith that the things we hope for will come into being because of our faith. Ambitious faith will knock down every challenge we face in life when we keep our eyes on Jesus and allow the power of the Holy Spirit to keep us close to God.

> Yet we know that a person is made right with God by faith in Jesus Christ, not by obeying the law. And we have believed in Christ Jesus, so that we might be made right with God because of our faith in Christ, not because we have obeyed the law. For no one will ever be made right with God by obeying the law. (Galatians 2:16 NLT)

Driven by Passion

You have something that moves you forward—a passion that brings you joy.

At times, our passions may dim, and we need a spark. When so, remember that God is completing his work in us. The power of the Holy Spirit will restore our passion and give us the energy to continue. As we remain open to His ways, we are reminded that we are successful through His power and patience.

> For God is working in you, giving you the desire and the power to do what pleases him. (Philippians 2:13 NLT)

I am redeemed through the blood of Jesus Christ. He loves me that much!

—DWC graduate

DECEMBER

I am lost.

Up until the age of eleven, I didn't know how my family was being affected by alcoholism or drug use. I was too busy being a child. I was sitting on my dad's kitchen counter, watching him make dinner and having one of our famous father-daughter talks. He said, "I don't ever want you to turn out like me."

I asked him what he meant by that. After talking with him some more, I realized he was talking about his drinking and drugging. I told him, "Daddy, you have nothing to worry about. I will not turn out like you. I'm going to change the world." I had such high hopes.

Four years later, my parents divorced, and my dad remarried. I was a fourteen-year-old girl, getting ready to start my freshman year in high school. I fell into a deep depression. It was that summer that I took my first drink. I remember not liking the taste, but it made me feel good inside. I didn't feel depressed, and I was able to put a smile on my face.

When I was twenty, I discovered I was pregnant with my daughter. I cleaned up my act and knew I was meant to be a mother. My daughter was an unexpected blessing, and I jumped into motherhood. I knew I wanted better for her. I didn't want her to be raised the way I was, but even my love for my child couldn't keep me from falling back into my old habit of drinking and partying. I would stay out all night and party while my husband was home with our daughter. Every time I was out drinking, I felt like a different person and as if my problems had disappeared. My husband and I started having arguments, as my parents had done. My addiction kept me from being a stable parent. My husband and I separated, and my daughter ended up living with her dad. I ended up living with a friend.

One night, my friend came home and said, "There is nothing left for me in Alaska. I'm moving back to Amarillo. You are welcome to come if you want."

It was at that moment that I knew I needed to escape. I hated life, my state, everything, and I wasn't happy. I called *one* person and said I was leaving. Once I was as far away from my parents as possible, I called home and let them know where I was going.

On December 22, 2003, three days before Christmas, we arrived in Amarillo, Texas. Nobody knew me; it was a fresh start. My fresh start didn't last long. Although I met some new friends, I still had the same old habits. I started going to bars, and I started drinking heavily again. I couldn't hold a job. I was dating this guy who introduced me to a "wonderful" drug called meth. Alcohol was not working for me anymore, and I needed something stronger. Although I knew better and should have run away from it, I was intrigued by it. This drug made me feel better than alcohol; this drug made me feel like I had more time in the day. I worked to support my drug habit.

My first run-in with the law wasn't for drinking or drugging; it was for theft. I had decided to go on a shopping spree with my checkbook and had written a bunch of bad checks. I was arrested and jailed and released on five years' probation. Shortly after being released from jail, I started using again.

Meth helped me stay awake at night so I could work the night shift; it also made me forget all my problems. I didn't feel depressed when I was on this drug. One day, when I had to report to my probation officer, she said she needed to do a drug test.

I knew I would come back dirty, and I didn't want to go back to jail. I said, "Save it. I need help."

I found myself in rehab. I spent thirty days in the facility, where I learned a lot and was given the tools I needed to live sober. Fourteen days after I got to rehab, my divorce from my husband was final. My boyfriend also broke up with me while I was in rehab. At the time, I thought it was the worst thing ever, but looking back, it was for the best.

After I left rehab, I moved into Martha's Home, a temporary homeless shelter for women to get back on their feet. While I was at Martha's Home, I put my name on the long list to get into the Downtown Women's Center. I was bound and determined to stay sober. My first serious test came when I was at Martha's Home. I was one hundred days sober when my grandma passed away. She was my number-one cheerleader. I went to her funeral in Alaska, sober. About a month after returning from the funeral, I started hanging out with my old boyfriend. I knew it would be trouble, and I wasn't thinking of using the tools I was given. I didn't care. A few days after we started hanging out, I relapsed for the first time. I ended up having to leave Martha's Home. I moved back in with my old boyfriend and his current girlfriend.

God must have been watching out for me. I made the decision that

I was done with this lifestyle. I left my boyfriend and left behind all my belongings. I went to a meeting and had no idea where I was going after that. I was somewhat prepared to sleep on the streets, but God sent a family to take me in and to let me stay with them until I was able to get into the Downtown Women's Center. This is a long-term shelter for women in recovery. When I started to work with the caseworker, I was very defiant and stubborn. I wanted to do things my way. I needed direction and help. I needed to learn how to navigate being a bipolar sober adult in this world. If I didn't, I was going to die.

I had been at DWC for about six months when I told my caseworker that I was moving in with a guy and would be leaving. She asked me if I had told the executive director. When I told her no, she took me to Diann's office.

I told Diann what I was doing, and she said, "*Oh no, you're not!*"

In 2008, I celebrated a year clean and sober. I celebrated that accomplishment by going out and getting high. There was a meeting at DWC on whether I would have to leave and what would happen. They gave me another chance. I was placed on house restriction for two weeks. The only place I was allowed to go was to work and meetings. I also had to write a paper.

I was almost at the end of my probation when I decided to play sick from work one day. I didn't go to the doctor until two days later, and I tried to change the date on the note. I got fired from my job. I wanted to move back home. It was time for me to be a mom, and I needed my family. I asked my probation officer if I could revoke my probation and do jail time. I served eight months in prison.

For years, I worked many dead-end jobs, and finally, I went to work for our school district. I started out working in Nutritional Services. Two years later, I became a paraprofessional (special education aide). Two years after that, I became a special education secretary. Finally, two years after that, I got and am now holding a three-year position as the support staff president for our union.

I've been married to my best friend for ten years. I am a mom to my daughter, and I'm a daughter to my parents. In my fourteen years of sobriety, I have had many ups and downs. I wouldn't be where I am today without a God who hasn't given up on me and who has always carried me.

I have been clean and sober since January 21, 2008. This did not happen overnight. I got to this point in my life with a lot of blood, sweat, tears, fighting every step of the way, Downtown Women's Center, AA, and a very loving God who never gave up on me.

I am a fighter!

December 1

God Sees Us

Diversity is a word often used as we choose to know others different from ourselves. Sometimes, we are unsure of those whose beliefs are different from ours. As Christ-followers, we believe God is the Creator of all. Love is also a choice. When we choose Jesus as our Savior, we are choosing love and acceptance as the way we see each other because of the way God sees us.

> The one who loves his brother or sister remains in the light, and there is no cause for stumbling in him. (1 John 2:10 CSB)

Unlimited Resources

Life often is lived as though we are deficient, not good enough. Material possessions become associated with happiness, and our values and emotions get mixed up. As faith people, we possess the peace in the middle of a storm. We believe God's love is more than enough. Abundance will flow into our spirits, and His faith will be ours.

> I pray that from his glorious, unlimited resources he will empower you with inner strength through his Spirit. Then Christ will make his home in your hearts as you trust in him. Your roots will grow down into God's love and keep you strong. (Ephesians 3:16–17 NLT)

December 3

Be Careful How You Live

Outward actions are a mirror of our inner thoughts and the way we live. Wisdom and understanding come to us by the Word of God and the power of the Holy Spirit. God's purpose for our lives will prevail, despite the challenges we face. We wake up each morning, knowing God will lead and guide us every day and in every way.

> So be careful how you live. Don't live like fools, but like those who are wise. Make the most of every opportunity in these evil days. Don't act thoughtlessly, but understand what the Lord wants you to do. (Ephesians 5:15–17 NLT)

A Heart of Good Soil

Tilling the soil before planting a crop involves turning over the soil to be ready to receive seed. For the Christ-followers, God prepares our hearts to receive and act on His truth. The Son will then shine on the good soil of our hearts. Our lives will be the proof of His goodness, which will stay with us as we bear the fruit of His Spirit.

> And the seed that fell on good soil represents those who hear and accept God's word and produce a harvest of thirty, sixty, or even a hundred times as much as had been planted! (Mark 4:20 NLT)

December 5

Everyone Who Asks Receives

An intimate line of communication opens up with God when we believe in the power of prayer. God promises that when we seek Him, we will find Him and know Him.

In prayer, begin with thankfulness for who He is and for all He has already provided you. Prayer can unlock the door to God's blessings, so knock. And don't be surprised by God's presence when you do.

> Ask, and it will be given to you; seek, and you will find; knock, and it will be opened to you. For everyone who asks receives, and he who seeks finds, and to him who knocks it will be opened. (Matthew 7:7–8 NKJV)

Hunger for His Truths

Throughout the centuries, people have explored the depths of the oceans and the vastness of space. Reading God's Word is the same. The more we read, the more we discover.

Give yourself permission to explore the endless depths of God's Word. The knowledge and wisdom you gain will give you a spiritual hunger for His truths that will never be satiated. Read on.

> The mind of the discerning acquires knowledge, and the ear of the wise seeks it. (Proverbs 18:15 CSB)

December 7

Nothing Is Impossible

A six-year-old was learning to ride her bike without training wheels. After weeks of trying, she was ready to give up, but she kept practicing. One day, her father said, "I think you are ready," and he gave her a push. Off she went, never looking back.

For us, even though we have a prayer life and even a study group, we may need a push from the Lord to go deeper and to reach out to show others a true life of faith. After all, sometimes, we all need a push.

> For nothing will be impossible for God. (Luke 1:37 NABRE)

God's Word Lives in Us

The Bible tells us in John 1 that the Word was in the beginning, the Word was with God, and the Word was God. Meditating on this passage shows His Word is alive and transformative. It is the power of God, prepared to soak into our lives below the surface, to penetrate to our core. In this way, the Word becomes alive in us in order to share God's goodness with others.

> For the word of God is living and powerful, and sharper than any two-edged sword, piercing even to the division of soul and spirit, and of joints and marrow and is a discerner of the thoughts and intents of the heart. (Hebrews 4:12 NKJV)

December 9

Prayer

The apostles asked Jesus to teach them how to pray as John the Baptist had taught his followers.

There is no secret recipe to prayer. God wants us to pray so that we can have our own personal relationships with him. God knows us better than we know ourselves. He already knows our needs. Sometimes, praying is more about sitting still and being quiet and trying to listen to what God is saying to us. Prayer gives us a chance to focus on what God wants for us and to help us realize that what we want may not be what He wants.

> Answer me when I call, my saving God. When troubles
> hem me in, set me free; take pity on me, hear my prayer.
> (Psalm 4:2 NABRE)

Persevere in Prayer

Receiving a life-threatening diagnosis or learning of a serious illness of a loved one shapes our faith in real time. This is when we cling tightly to the hope of faith, alive through us. Our faith continues to be fresh as we learn to adapt our faith in all kinds of easy and hard situations.

> Rejoice in hope, endure in affliction, persevere in prayer.
> (Romans 12:12 NABRE)

December 11

We Will Know What to Say

Sharing our faith in Jesus Christ with others may seem overwhelming. Not sure of what to say, sometimes we become hesitant. As we allow Jesus to be the Lord of our lives, we will find our words and know what to say. Taking a second to pray before we share about the faith within us can pave the way. The Holy Spirit will give us the ability to be gentle and kind as we tell others about the goodness of the Lord.

> Instead, you must worship Christ as Lord of your life. And if someone asks about your hope as a believer, always be ready to explain it. But do this in a gentle and respectful way. Keep your conscience clear. Then if people speak against you, they will be ashamed when they see what a good life you live because you belong to Christ. (1 Peter 3:15–16 NLT)

Surprise Blessings

Generosity is a true part of Jesus. He teaches us to take on His heart and His generous spirit.

Have you ever been surprised to receive an unexpected blessing? When you give to others, do so with a generous heart. Do so because the Lord has blessed you. This is a spiritual "pass it on."

> But when you do a charitable deed, do not let your left hand know what your right hand is doing, that your charitable deed may be in secret; and your Father who sees in secret will Himself reward you openly. (Matthew 6:3–4 NKJV)

Come and Be Welcomed by Him

Sometimes we are pulled in different directions by people and events. We may struggle to pay attention to those close to us. We know that Jesus was focused on those who were seeking Him. He ministered to their healing, taught them, and welcomed them to the kingdom.

Look to Him to improve your service to others—teaching, comforting, and, most of all, showing your loving spirit.

> The crowds, meanwhile, learned of this and followed him.
> He received them and spoke to them about the kingdom
> of God, and he healed those who needed to be cured.
> (Luke 9:11 NABRE)

Held by His Hand

If you've ever watched a travel program of a wilderness journey across barren land, you appreciate the comforts of your home more.

The Christian life is not absent of challenges. The Christian life is about the faith to continue on, to break through. The going through can encourage an intimate fellowship with God.

You can count on the truth. He will never leave you, especially during the most difficult of times.

> The valiant one whose steps are guided by the Lord, who will delight in his way, May stumble, but he will never fall, for the Lord holds his hand. (Psalm 37:23–24 NABRE)

December 15

In Awe of God's Love and Mercy

Have you ever felt put down, even dismissed? If so, you can lean hard into God for true comfort. He will lead, guide, and reveal His plans for you. This shows you His love and His mercy. In Him, there is a weaving of comfort available to you. You are valued and highly praised.

> But as for me, I will come into Your house in the multitude of Your mercy; In fear of You I will worship toward Your holy temple. Lead me, O Lord, in your righteousness because of my enemies; Make Your way straight before my face. (Psalm 5:7–8 NKJV)

Living by Faith

Not everyone will accept us at all times and in all ways. Sometimes, we must accept ourselves first. This is what it means to say, "We live by faith." Faith in the Lord is faith in the One who accepts us. By accepting ourselves, we show our acceptance of others. This is how we live each day—with promise.

> For I am not ashamed of the gospel of Christ, for it is the power of God to salvation for everyone who believes, for the Jew first and also for the Greek. For in it the righteousness of God is revealed from faith to faith; as it is written, "The just shall live by faith." (Romans 1:16–17 NKJV)

December 17

A Glorious Promise

We are a part of the promise God has given us and wants us to know. He cares for us and wants His peace to be our peace. The challenge is how to move that promise into a central part of our lives and the lives of our families. We are promised that His promise is true and real.

> Now we, brethren, as Isaac was, are children of promise. (Galatians 4:28 NKJV)

Be Kind

"You can catch more flies with honey than with vinegar" is a saying many of us have heard.

Sometimes, when we come across an unpleasant person, we may show unkindness. This is not the way of a Christ-follower. Our way, God's way, is to surround this person with love, patience, and kindness. Humility, directed by the Holy Spirit, speaks louder than words of correction or condemnation. Ask God each day for the wisdom to walk, talk, and live in His grace.

> A servant of the Lord must not quarrel but must be kind to everyone, be able to teach, and be patient with difficult people. Gently instruct those who oppose the truth. Perhaps God will change those people's hearts, and they will learn the truth. (2 Timothy 2:24–25 NLT)

December 19

It's Not All about Me

All we have to do is look at traffic to see different personality styles. Many people seem to think, "It's all about me." If we are honest, "me" may be on our minds more than we would like to think. Don't be discouraged, though. As we adjust our outlooks to be more like Jesus, we train our minds as well. In this way, we become less concerned with the differences in others and more concerned with respecting and loving everyone.

Direct my heart toward your testimonies and away from gain. (Psalm 119:36 NABRE)

Through Faith, We Receive Grace

It isn't easy being a Christ-follower when we are young in the faith. We each are given the room to grow in our faith, expanding our circles of love and acceptance to include those new to us and those we have known for a long time. As we grow and become stronger in our faith actions, we receive the grace to allow others to be themselves, each to grow into faith in their own ways.

> For the grace of God has been revealed, bringing salvation
> to all people. (Titus 2:11 NLT)

December 21

Living a Life of Goodness

In a larger society, we understand there are rules and guidelines. The kingdom of God is different. As believers, we show others God's love in how we live and make decisions, and we include others in our prayer and worship lives. A community of faith is brought together not around rules but goodness, the same goodness with which God has blessed us all. This is a more satisfying way.

> For the Kingdom of God is not a matter of what we eat or drink, but of living a life of goodness and peace and joy in the Holy Spirit. If you serve Christ with this attitude, you will please God, and others will approve of you, too. (Romans 14:17–18 NLT)

Commit and Trust

There are many parts of us and our lives to which we commit every day. Going to work, taking kids to school, and helping a neighbor can all make up our day. What would our lives be like if we made the same commitments to God? Committing to and trusting in the Lord is backed by His promise of lowering our fears and fulfilling our hopes. Our part is to commit and trust. His part is to be with us on each school bus, in each conference room meeting, or fixing that stuck door for a neighbor—no part is too small for the Lord to be with us.

> Commit your way to the Lord, trust also in Him, and He shall bring it to pass. (Psalm 37:5 NKJV)

Believe

During the holiday time of year, movies, music, and stores encourage us to believe that Santa Claus is on his way. It is good to know our God is a twelve-months-a-year God. He is always available. His grace and mercy are the perfect gifts. Our belief in Him will reward us with the blessings of this season and all seasons to come.

> And it is impossible to please God without faith. Anyone who wants to come to him must believe that God exists and that he rewards those who sincerely seek him. (Hebrews 11:6 NLT)

Christmas Eve

Christmas Eve is special, as we anticipate celebrating the day Jesus was born. There is excitement in the air as we look forward to worship, celebrations, and spending time with family and friends. Many of us get to experience gathering with loved ones at this time, but some do not. Living away from family or having to work can be difficult, and the traditions we look forward to can be changed or diminished.

Wherever you are on this happy day, know that you carry the true message of Christ with you always. Wherever you live, work, worship, or celebrate the birth of Jesus, this message is a gift to us all. Bring the message with you and share it with others, wherever you are today.

> For, At just the right time Christ will be revealed from heaven by the blessed and only almighty God, the King of all kings and Lord of all lords. (1 Timothy 6:15 NLT)

December 25

Make Room for Jesus

The birth of Christ is to be celebrated. We may listen to someone read this biblical story on Christmas Eve or Christmas Day. Remember the innkeeper when you listen to the reading. He showed compassion by making room in the stable for Mary to give birth. When we make room for Jesus, we are different, better people.

> So it was, that while they were there, the days were completed for her to be delivered. And she brought forth her firstborn Son, and wrapped Him in swaddling cloths, and laid Him in a manger, because there was no room for them in the inn. (Luke 2:6–7 NKJV)

Stillness

Tranquility is experienced in the early morning silence. Christ is with us in the stillness as well as in the noise. Whether quiet and still or walking fast in the midst of a noisy day, Christ is with us. He speaks His heart. We open our ears and minds to listen.

> Be still, and know that I am God; I will be exalted among the nations, I will be exalted in the earth. (Psalm 46:10 NKJV)

December 27

Fill Me with Wisdom and Understanding

Everyone has desires. Most of us just want to pay our bills and have a little left at the end of the month. As believers in Jesus Christ, we desire to be filled with His wisdom and have understanding of God's plan for our lives. It is right to have a desire for God's wisdom as a guide to live our daily lives to the fullest. These are right and good desires.

> So we have not stopped praying for you since we first heard about you. We ask God to give you complete knowledge of his will and to give you spiritual wisdom and understanding. Then the way you live will always honor and please the Lord, and your lives will produce every kind of good fruit. All the while, you will grow as you learn to know God better and better. (Colossians 1:9–10 NLT)

Flourish in His Word

Spiritual growth takes place as we allow the Holy Spirit to flow over us with His wisdom. As we read His Word, we accept the Lord's character for ourselves. God's Word becomes planted deep within us. The truth of His Word soaks our spirit and gives us the desire to be always faithful. Think of God's Word while fixing breakfast or taking an after-work walk. By practicing our faith, our lives will flourish.

> But his delight is in the law of the Lord, And in his law he meditates day and night. He shall be like a tree Planted by the rivers of water, That brings forth its fruit in its season, Whose leaf also shall not wither; And whatever he does shall prosper. (Psalm 1:2–3 NKJV)

December 29

Rejoice and Be Glad

Receiving an unexpected gift can bring excitement, especially in young children. Their eyes light up the moment they receive their gift. This same joy can be a daily smile on the face of the believer. Live, determined to maintain that childlike joy each day, each evening—and smile the smile of faith.

Rejoice in the Lord always. Again I will say, rejoice!
(Philippians 4:4 NKJV)

New Nature

The lessons learned in life come from having an experience that may create change in our beliefs. If we do not adjust our thoughts or beliefs, life will be out of balance.

Let the Word of God move your spirit and replace the old way of thinking with the nature of His life-giving wisdom and love.

> Since you have heard about Jesus and have learned the truth that comes from him, throw off your old sinful nature and your former way of life, which is corrupted by lust and deception. Instead, let the Spirit renew your thoughts and attitudes. Put on your new nature, created to be like God—truly righteous and holy. (Ephesians 4:21–24 NLT)

December 31

New Day Dawning

As another year draws to a close, a new day is dawning. Now is the time to let the troubles of the past take their rightful place, knowing God is turning difficulties into goodness. Look for God's goodness in all the challenges you faced this year. As you do, you will find that every challenge was conquered by the love of Jesus Christ.

> I have told you these things, so that in me you may have peace. In this world you will have trouble. But take heart! I have overcome the world. (John 16:33 NIV)

Amen

I am loved by my Lord and Savior, Jesus Christ.

—DWC graduate

INSPIRING STORIES

I am unsure of my identity.

Once I got in recovery and started peeling back the pieces of my life, I understood, with clarity, why I became a drug addict.

My mother, my father, my mother's ex-husband, and my siblings and I all lived under the same roof at our home in California. I was molested there at a very young age by my mother's ex-husband. It went on until I was around seven years old. My family dealt with it in very unhealthy ways, once it was brought to light. To this day, I still don't quite understand why my father didn't kill this man in my defense. My mother did a lot of manipulation to keep the peace. I was told that he did more for me than my own dad did, so when it came time to tell the truth, I lied to cover up for him and please my mom. My secret was shoved under the rug and never spoken of again. I thought I wouldn't be loved if I told on him. That man was there for me at all my events and games and took me to church. Secrets kept me sick. I knew something was wrong, but I couldn't put my finger on it.

I covered up my pain and confusion by excelling in everything I did. I suppressed it all. When I started dating, I lost my virginity to the first boyfriend I had. I didn't start drinking until later in high school, and I smoked cigarettes and pot for fun. I liked the way it made me feel. I stopped going to church and let go of the sports I was playing. I wanted the attention I got from the world when I would party. One of my friends from high school told me about crystal meth. I was going to be in a friend's wedding and wanted to look my best; she said it would help me lose weight quickly. It changed me. Everything was so *alive.*

I moved to Arizona with my boyfriend. I went hard with the meth and tried every drug known to humans. It wasn't long before my parents got a phone call in California, telling them that I was out of control. They drove to Arizona to pick me up. I was clueless about addiction and thought I was just experimenting. My boyfriend returned home, and I jumped headfirst back into our toxic relationship. We lived in garages and used the bathroom in buckets. I was beaten with a two-by-four. My mom called the pastor from the church where I grew up, and together, they made arrangements for me to move in with the pastor's daughters in San Diego to get away from the drug scene.

Who knew that the daughters were partying too? I thought I was OK because I wasn't doing meth anymore, but I drank heavily and went to the clubs. One time, the other girls went back home without me for the weekend. I decided to stay because I had a plan. I met up with some guys I knew from the marine base. We did some meth, and things got out of control. The girls came back, and somehow, my parents were called once again. "Your daughter is on meth here in San Diego." I was shipped back to my parents and found out I had been pregnant with my boyfriend's child the whole time. We decided as a family that I should have an abortion.

I started questioning my own identity and asked myself almost every day, "Who are you, anyway?" I started hanging out with a group of Hispanic friends who were tough guys, and I wanted to be one of them. I started dressing like they did and acting as they did, and I fell right into their culture. I told them all I was part Hispanic, with my dark hair and olive complexion. I didn't want to be a part of my race anymore. I loved the attention I got from the tough crowd. I was a gangster, hanging out with bald guys with tattoos and big, baggy clothes. I slowly became another person with another persona. Bright colors began to adorn the painting of my life. I told myself I was Hispanic for twenty-plus years.

I went toward energy, the negative energy. I never did anything illegal. I believe the Lord had His hand upon me. I got into a relationship with a Hispanic man. We went to many concerts, and I learned to cook with his family. We used meth together, and I became addicted to the intense feelings I would have during meth. I knew it was wrong, but I liked it. The drugs intensified everything. When this man cheated on me, I had had it with broken hearts. Again, my identity was questioned, and I didn't know where I belonged. I started pushing meth hard into my body. I was broken. I began to accept whatever treatment people gave to me.

My baby brother moved to Amarillo, Texas, to get away from the gangs. We had a friend whose pastor had come to the Nazarene church in Amarillo. They invited my brother, and my mom agreed to send him. She, of course, blamed me for his behavior, which was not conducive to an honest life. I missed my brother tremendously, but my parents did not want me to influence him any longer. I went to Amarillo by bus in 1998 to celebrate his birthday. He picked me up at the bus stop, and my first words were, "Where are we? Where are the lowriders? Where are all the Mexicans? Where are the mountains and water?"

He said plainly, "We are not doing that anymore."

My brother lived with a bunch of roommates in a beautiful home. We went to a bar because drinking for him was still OK. I felt entirely out of place. I looked for a reason to fight and was rude to everyone around me. He begged me just to chill out.

The culture in Amarillo was so very different from what I was used to back home. I got a job and decided to stay in Amarillo. I planned to stay for the summer, make some money, and go back home. A friend at work showed one of my fly pictures to a guy who worked with her husband. My future husband came into my life, and I was never the same. The chase began, and I played hard to get. He was Mexican, but he was a working guy. There was something different about him, and I fell head over heels. *Everything* was different with him. He made me feel things I had never before experienced.

We got pregnant right away and went to California to tell my parents we were getting married. Upon our return to Texas, I found out that he had another woman in his life, and they had three children together. I was devastated. I told him that I would bow out—he had more to lose if he lost them and not me. In everyone's eyes, I was the home-wrecker. My infatuation for him and my obsession with how he made me feel took center stage, and I welcomed him back into my home and my bed. He played us both for years. He must have loved us fighting over him, considering we were pregnant at the same time.

My parents asked me to come home, but I wanted my child to know his father. That wasn't at all true. I just wanted to keep my man and have his baby. So many women get sucked into that lie.

I started using drugs like mad. I would get out of bed in the middle of the night when someone would knock on my door, leave my baby in the crib asleep, and party until the sun came up. It was a vicious cycle. I still do not recall how my rent got paid, how the lights stayed on, or how we survived. I was not raising my son right, and all I could think about was how to keep this man in my life. I used daily to forget that he wasn't mine. We were both narcissistic and a certain kind of ugly, so it worked in a very sick and depraved way.

When my son was starting kindergarten, I realized I needed to do something different with my life. My man was in prison. I started going to college, moved into Martha's Home, got involved in church, and was a great soccer mom, but in reality, I was just off a binge. While at Martha's Home, I used pain pills for a kidney infection and started using them like candy. They had no idea I was abusing my medication.

I was ready to get some closure in my family and decided to go back to California to confront my dad about why he hadn't protected me from the sexual abuse I had endured. It was time to face reality. My mom said, "When are you going to let this go?" I didn't make it to California; my dad was killed in a car accident before I could catch a bus. I knew exactly what would make me feel better—meth. I went back to what felt good and coped the only way I knew how. I functioned better on the pain pills than on the meth and wanted to finish school, so I justified using the pills. I was stumbling into the web of deceit that wrapped me up and threatened my life. I got married during this time to my man, who was in prison, and I couldn't believe I finally got what I wanted. He was coming home to our family and *me*, and I was elated.

He got a great job in the oilfield in Odessa, Texas, so we moved. I was so mean and hateful to him. Breaking things and cutting him with words felt so good. I was full of anger and malice. He took everything I threw at him. I wanted to hurt him the way I had been hurt. I tested him constantly, and he continued to stay. I believed him when he said he had gotten saved in prison. The oilfield industry went south, and we went back to Amarillo. I was so afraid I would lose control over him in this city. I started back on the pain pills, taking thirty a day. I stole from every neighbor in my neighborhood. I stole from everyone to stay high.

I ended up pregnant with my second son. I stopped taking the drugs and got very sick from withdrawal on top of morning sickness. Once he was born, I suffered from postpartum depression. I despised my child and didn't even want to be around him. I couldn't love him; I didn't know how to. Everyone I turned to for help just kept me at arm's length. I begged my husband for some dope and threatened him if he refused. He was so done with me and didn't know how to deal with me, so he did. He asked me for some, and I sure didn't care if he got high with me or not. He hasn't stopped to this day.

I don't like to say that I am a victim, but meth is like a brew from the darkness. Meth is so evil, and there are evil spirits attached to it. I almost ended up in a mental institution after trying to hang myself. My thoughts were no longer my own. My husband became a person of the darkness. My husband was gaslighting and manipulating me by psychological means into questioning my sanity. The meth opened doors that shouldn't have been opened; we lived in the shadows. I didn't want to die when I tried to hang myself; I just wanted to die to my feelings. Betrayal was rampant in my home, and secrets became exciting. Isn't that what I learned as a child? The betrayal was exciting, and it took us over.

On December 2, 2012, my husband left. Christmas has always been my escape, no matter the season of life I was in. I would decorate to the nines, no matter where I was in the space in my head. It made me feel like a child, and my childhood was taken away from me. It gave me such joy. That year, it was ruined. There were no presents under the tree for the kids. The boys and I still decided to keep the tree up and celebrate without him. He wasn't going to take away my joy during that holiday. We made it work, and it was beautiful.

I surfed the rocky oceans of life for the next four years. I stayed in hotels, motels, and even my car with my boys. We would stay with friends here and there, and I stayed in denial. The church I attended and used as a means to escape always knew when I stopped using because I would grace them once again with my presence. I kept allowing my husband back in; what I allowed continued.

I started using again on my own and tore our little efficiency apartment to shreds from floor to ceiling because I was so strung out every day, and paranoia and hallucinations had me seeing things that weren't there. My sons would come home from school to find me coloring the red light on the TV. At one point, I thought my son was out to get me, and I contemplated stabbing him.

In August 2015, I miraculously awoke from my psychosis and told myself that I needed to get real help. I was running out of money for food, rent, and bills. I reached out to every person I knew, including my pastor, and no one was responding. Didn't they love me? Care for my kids and me? Want the best for me? Why wouldn't they help me? I had burned every bridge on my path to destruction. The spirit of suicide came upon me once again.

I had an epiphany. I needed to go to the Downtown Women's Center and find this woman named Donna, whom I had met while in Martha's Home. I didn't even know what the Downtown Women's Center was, but I knew I needed to get there—now.

I went there looking pretty wretched. Shannon was sitting at the desk. I said, "I need help. I need Donna."

"Sweetheart, Donna isn't here. Is there something I can help you with?"

"I will only talk to Donna," I replied.

"Can you please wait one minute?"

Diann came out to talk to me, and I reluctantly went into her office. I know the Holy Spirit was speaking through this angelic voice coming from the woman sitting across from me.

"I will call Donna for you, but can you please tell me what is going on?"

"I need help. I have two children and they stay with me—they are staying with me. I have a sack of drugs at home."

Diann said, "Do everything that we ask, and we will have your back to the fullest."

I needed instant gratification, and I wasn't getting it. She asked me to come back that afternoon, but there was no room for gaps in my day, as far as I was concerned. I went to get my older son and took him with me back to the DWC, where Donna met me at the door. We came up with a plan for me to turn myself in and sit out my time in jail for some tickets. She also told me to do exactly what they asked of me, and they would have my back to the fullest. Something told me to believe her, and they would love me. It was music to my ears. My pastor and his wife took my son into their home. I flushed the sack of dope at my house. I slept harder than I ever had. The only thing I packed up in my apartment was my Christmas decorations. Those boxes were going with me, no matter what. I sat out two weeks in Randall County after letting the church know of our plans and what was about to take place. When I left my boys with the pastor, I heard these words from a kind person in the congregation: "You are brave and courageous for doing this."

The Downtown Women's Center was still unsure of what to do with my boys and me when I came out of jail. I threw a tantrum because I wasn't getting what I wanted when I wanted it. I got a call two hours later. Donna said, "I have spoken with Diann. What we are about to do has been on our hearts. We have had a vision for mothers and their children who need recovery but weren't sure how to see it to fruition. We are opening the Abba House for you and your sons."

God used me to be the first one, their trial run of women with children. I bypassed Haven House, and we all learned how to do this together. I got on my knees in the Abba House. I started praying aloud while my younger son was asleep in the bed. I started praying, "Lord, is this where you will have me be? Is this what you want from me?"

I heard a sweet voice from across the room say, "Yes."

It was so simple and so touching that Jesus would speak audibly to me through my sleeping son. I needed that more than I needed breath in my lungs.

God is working in my life today and making me who I was always supposed to be. I put down the other personas that I had taken on to fit in. I am starting to see God's purpose for me and who I really am. I am *outrageous*! I am full of color still today and can communicate with so many different groups of people. What the enemy meant for harm, God meant for His good and His glory. The Lord found something special and had His hand on me. I was weak, like a baby with milk. During my wanderings, I hadn't tasted the meat and the fruit of His Word. Only now, in this season, I started to remind myself that it is OK to say that I am Caucasian, not Hispanic, but then the Lord said to me, "Color does not matter; you are my child."

I have grown so much. I have four years of being clean and sober, and I work at a recovery center, helping people in trouble. I am a counselor for the Lord and give people an anchor of hope. The rain will fall, the wind will blow, and I am an anchor in the storm of others. It is for the glory of God. Today, I work with probation and deal with people daily who have been in gangs and were just like me. I have found that broken people are constantly seeking something to help them know who they are in the world. The enemy of our souls uses that to his advantage and plays on our identity crises. I am grateful that the seeds of the Word were planted inside me at a young age. Not all people can say that. I am a light to others who the world has thrown away.

I am fearfully and wonderfully made!

I am codependent.

My journey into the darkness of addiction began when I was very young. My father was an alcoholic but had gotten sober before my memories began. I never saw him dive into a bottle, but his addiction eventually caught up to him, and he ended up on the liver transplant list. Cirrhosis had eaten him up. After a long five-year wait, he received his new liver in 1999. When he had the transplant, cancer had already spread throughout his entire body, and they gave him only six months to live, which is exactly how long he stayed on this earth. Because of the daily pain I saw him in, I made an inner vow never to use drugs or drink.

Not long after my father's death, I met my husband and patched the gaping hole in my heart with a new love. We were together for seventeen years. He was an addict, and I was unaware. I was so gullible and naïve to what was happening around me. I had no idea that my husband lived a separate life apart from my heart's desire. I got pregnant, my husband ended up in prison, and I had to come to some harsh truths about my life. When he was released, he went right back to using and left me feeling very alone and isolated.

If you can't beat them, join them. I started using meth, desperately trying to understand my husband's heart. I could stop on a dime and would go months without using. However, the codependent yoke wrapped tightly around my neck was my driving force. My moods and days depended solely on his. My husband's father passed away in 2014. Before his death, he had blessed our family with $25,000 of our inheritance. I just knew that a normal life was on the horizon. We could finally afford comfortable living arrangements and could settle down, but every last dime went to drugs, and our addiction took a hazardous turn.

People were in and out of our house; our front door was revolving. I wanted out so badly, but I still held tightly to the dream of being a good housewife, mother, and member of society. The yoke tightened, and I relied solely on dreams to get by and forgot about my reality. I finally threw my hands up in the air and walked out on my entire family. My husband had our younger son for close to eight months, my mom had our older son, and I lived with my brother. We were still addicts, but our marriage had been destroyed. We were both still high on a daily basis, just in separate homes.

Child Protective Services (CPS) was called, and they were at my mom's door the following day. She contacted me, and I watched my life crumble around me. It was like watching a movie play out in slow motion. The CPS worker told my mom that someone had mentioned in the report that we were smoking dope around our children. I knew it wasn't me. I smoked only at my brother's home. I desperately wanted to come clean to the CPS worker and get it off my chest that I was unable to stop using. I wanted to be released from the prison I was in but could not bear to come clean in front of my mom. I took the CPS worker to the side and spilled the beans about my sad, depressing life. She asked me to get my younger son's things together so he could be placed with my mom.

I left to meet my husband at his home. I told him what was happening and that I was instructed to take our baby boy to my mother's house with his things, and within minutes, the two of us were smoking the pipe. I couldn't believe that even the thought of my children being taken wasn't enough for me to stay clean. At that moment, I knew something had to change, and I needed to get real help for my situation.

For a long time, I blamed my husband for what was happening. CPS tested both of my boys for methamphetamines. My older son had just a small amount of meth in his system; my younger son tested three times higher than me, and I was a daily smoker. The meth had gone through his tiny pores, and he was high on a daily basis. I have never felt so low in all my life. I realized we had slowly been killing our children.

CPS recommended that we both go to rehab. I looked for an excuse to leave. We bounced between rehabs before I finally found the Downtown Women's Center.

I have never felt such peace in my life as I do today because of the program at the DWC. They allowed me to come in, broken and ashamed. It wasn't long before I was able to complete my services with CPS and regain custody of my boys, and we moved into the Abba House. The Downtown Women's Center loved me back to life until I could love myself enough to finally rip off my coat of shame and my yoke of codependency. I am codependent no more. We have a beautiful apartment at the Gratitude House now, and I am entirely free from the lifestyle that tore my family apart.

I am in the process of getting a divorce from a man who could not and would not get his life together. He still uses drugs, and I stay far away from him. My sons mean the world to me; my home is a place of peace and rest. They need their mother to be strong and courageous, and for the first time in my life, I can say that I am just that. It took a long time for me to find forgiveness, not for others but for myself. The counseling I receive, the meetings I attend, the steps that I work, and the love of the Lord—these have led me to a place I didn't think existed for me.

I am forgiven!

AUTHORS AND EDITORS

Thank you to Sharon Miner for her inspiration and motivation to create this book. Sharon has spent her life spiritually coaching women as they pursue a life of recovery. She also has been a leadership coach and a Bible teacher. Supported by her husband, Jerry, and her son, Shawn, Sharon makes her home in Amarillo, Texas.

It was through Sharon's ability to listen to these broken women who passed through our program and hear what they were saying that she was able to give them a voice. Their stories show the world that they are worthy of being redeemed.

Thank you to the staff and the board of directors for their input. This book would not have been possible without their service and dedication.

Thank you to Diann Gilmore, Jack Hilton, Roy Bowen, Hollis Parker, Susan Barros, Ann Hicks, and Julie Ballard for their long hours of dedication to the writing and editing of *Everyone Is Redeemable: Daily Devotional.*

Printed in the United States
by Baker & Taylor Publisher Services